Supporting
and
Sustaining
Teachers'
Professional
Development

Supporting
and
Sustaining
Teachers'
Professional
Development

A Principal's Guide

MARILYN TALLERICO

CORWIN PRESS
A SAGE Publications Company
Thousand Oaks, California

For information:

Corwin Press
A Sage Publications Company
2455 Teller Road
Thousand Oaks, California 91320
www.corwinpress.com

Sage Publications Ltd.
1 Oliver's Yard
55 City Road
London EC1Y 1SP
United Kingdom

Sage Publications India Pvt. Ltd.
B-42, Panchsheel Enclave
Post Box 4109
New Delhi 110 017 India

Printed in the United States of America.

Library of Congress Cataloging-in-Publication Data

Tallerico, Marilyn.
Supporting and sustaining teachers' professional development: A principal's guide / Marilyn Tallerico.
       p. cm.
Includes bibliographical references and index.
ISBN 1-4129-1334-9 (cloth)—ISBN 1-4129-1335-7 (pbk.)
   1. Teachers—Inservice training. 2. Teachers—Professional relationships.
3. School management and organization. I. Title.
LB1731.T26 2005
370'.71'55—dc22   2004024082

This book is printed on acid-free paper.

05   06   07   08   09   10   8   7   6   5   4   3   2   1

Acquisitions Editor:	Elizabeth Brenkus
Editorial Assistant:	Candice L. Ling
Production Editor:	Laureen A. Shea
Copy Editor:	Terese Platten, Freelance Editorial Services
Typesetter:	C&M Digitals (P) Ltd.
Proofreader:	Colleen Brennan
Indexer:	Nara Wood
Cover Designer:	Michael Dubowe
Graphic Designer:	Anthony Paular

Contents

List of Tables

List of Figures

Preface

This book is for busy school principals: principals who want to support and challenge their teachers but for whom the urgent keeps getting in the way of the important; principals who know they should be instructional leaders but whose days are quickly filled with emergencies, operations, student discipline, community relations, phone calls, and meetings; principals who believe in research-based best practices, but who do not have time to read volumes or spend days attending conferences.

How will this book help? By doing three things. First, it will provide practical suggestions for supporting and facilitating teachers' professional development; suggestions that are both big-picture and doable, strategic and immediately actionable; suggestions that assume the principal will not be the one leading every initiative, but will need to know how to decide among varied approaches, how to plan, share leadership, stay focused on student learning, and make multiple initiatives cohere.

Second, this book will succinctly synthesize the research and theory behind those suggestions. It will explain *why*, in readable and easily digestible ways. It will provide rationales that principals can use to explain and justify their school's professional development foci to governing boards, communities, outside funding agencies, and anyone else concerned with the reasoning behind the choices.

Third, this book will link teachers' professional development to student learning. These links are what can build both teachers' and communities' support for the school's professional development directions. That support is critical to the development efforts' progress because neither the suggested actions nor the rationale will be heeded without it.

In sum, actionable strategies grounded in sound rationale and connected to student learning are the three aids this book provides.

Distinctiveness

How is this book different from the many others on the market that address staff development? First, it focuses on interpreting current national standards for professional development and applying them specifically to the work of school leaders. Second, rather than including detailed elaboration of each and every standard, this book is intentionally selective. It centers, instead, on seven key questions whose answers capture what current and aspiring principals most need to know about using the standards to improve their schools. I know of no other resource that is as compact, focused, and readable enough to help busy educators stay up-to-date on expert thinking and best practices for supporting teachers' on-the-job development.

Additionally, this book appends a handy glossary to acquaint readers with terms that often surface in this and other resources relevant to professional development. And, for readers who wish to pursue any of the topics mentioned in greater depth or detail, a contemporary reference list is also included.

Description of the Book

What, more specifically, will you find in this volume? National standards for professional development center on three essential elements: content, process, and context (National Staff Development Council, 2001). This book is organized into three parts consistent with those standards. Additionally, each chapter is constructed around a question fundamental to school leadership.

For example, Part I includes two chapters, both centered on means of determining what the substance (content) of a school's professional development efforts should be. Chapter 1, "How Should Adult and Student Learning Be Linked?" explains and illustrates simple data analysis techniques for homing in on gaps between where students are and where you would like them to be. It challenges school leaders to move away from traditional paper-and-pencil surveys of teachers' needs or interests toward more student-driven focusing of adult learning content.

Chapter 2 introduces five distinct ways of thinking about evaluating professional development initiatives. It suggests steps principals can take to use evaluation results to adjust and refine adult learning content. To help avoid the common pitfall of flitting from one hot topic to another, Chapters 1 and 2 together reinforce strategies for solidly connecting teachers' professional development to your school's top priorities for student learning.

Whereas Part I is focused on the *what* of adult learning, Part II examines the *how* (process). Chapter 3, "Which Models Best Suit Your Goals?" identifies five fundamental designs that all school leaders should be familiar with: Individually Guided, Collaborative Problem Solving, Observation and Assessment of Teaching, Training, and Action Research. This chapter succinctly summarizes the rationale for each model and offers ideas for deciding among design options. Its companion chapter in Part II addresses the question, "What do we know about effective staff development practices?" It synthesizes state-of-the art thinking to bring you up-to-date on the most salient aspects of the knowledge base relevant to school leaders. Regardless of the models you and your teachers determine to be most appropriate for your school, this growing body of research on best practice will help you plan, implement, and sustain improvements in your adult learning programs.

Importantly, neither strong content (Part I) nor well-grounded design (Part II) alone will ensure the success of teachers' professional development in schools. Favorable systemic conditions are also required. Accordingly, Part III, "Creating Supportive Contexts," addresses three questions integral to establishing and maintaining nurturing environments for adult learning. Chapter 5, "How Can Leaders Focus Improvement Efforts?" centers on setting clear direction and integrating multiple innovations. Together, these actions can increase coherence and decrease the fragmentation and overload that so often plague professional development and school improvement initiatives. Chapter 6, "How Are More Enabling Cultures Shaped?" describes strategies for communication and everyday acts of leadership that foster favorable contexts for adult and student learning. This chapter also challenges conventional notions about teacher resistance to change, instead encouraging attention to the school structures and systemic conditions that support the status quo. Two key resources—time and funding—are the focus of Chapter 7, "How Can Resources Be Optimized?"

A brief concluding chapter wraps up and reinforces salient messages for school-based administrative leadership of teachers' professional development. It is followed by a glossary and list of references. Consistent with the approach taken throughout the book, the appended resources were chosen for their relevance to current and aspiring principals.

Summary and Use

Three premises underlie this volume. First, student learning is the goal and the desired end. Continuous teacher growth and development is but one of several means toward that end.

Second, there are more similarities than differences between adult learning and student learning. If savvy administrators emphasize and capitalize on the similarities, teacher and community ownership will follow more readily. And shared ownership increases the odds of long-term commitment, follow-up, and collective responsibility for improving student learning.

Third, leadership matters. Every school has numerous and varied programs, goals, special projects, partnerships, and hopes. Principals are in a unique position to see and understand how each contributes to—or detracts from—the whole. With that needed perspective comes responsibility for big picture sense making, focus, prioritizing, and oversight.

In sum, school-based administrative support and guidance are key to building coherence among multiple improvement initiatives. And important among those initiatives is teachers' professional development.

Audience and Other Uses for This Book

The primary audience for this volume is current and prospective PreK–12 principals, assistant principals, and other school building leaders (e.g., department chairs, grade-level heads). Prospective includes students in college and university educational leadership preparation programs—the future pool of school administrators.

Professors of educational leadership will find this book's contents a welcome blend of theoretical and practical insights, addressing needs to expose prospective administrators to multiple perspectives while satisfying graduate students' interest in concrete action and understandable illustrations. This volume can be used as a supplementary text in courses such as "School Personnel Administration," "Human Resources Management," "The Principalship," "Leadership for Adult Learning," "Professional Development in Schools" or "Foundations of Educational Administration."

Staff development committees, school improvement planning teams, teachers, central office administrators, curriculum coordinators, educational consultants, and school board members will also find this book accessible and useful. These audiences will likely appreciate the broad overview of best practices for professional development. They will also increase their understanding of why and how generic strategies need to be tailored to each school's uniqueness.

A Final Thought

The continuous growth of students and staff has always been central to the vision of strong school leaders. Recent state policy directions and the federal No Child Left Behind Act of 2001 further increase administrative responsibility for improving student achievement, retaining highly qualified teachers, and grounding school practices in sound research. This book is a useful resource for all leaders concerned with exercising those responsibilities well.

Acknowledgments

I am indebted to the researchers, practitioners, and professional associations whose studies, insights, and perspectives helped inform this work. Special, heartfelt appreciation is also extended to Chris Ritter and Joan N. Burstyn for their unwavering personal support and encouragement. I am grateful to Interim Dean Emily Robertson and Program Chair Joseph B. Shedd of Syracuse University for supporting the sabbatical leave that facilitated this project. Finally, I wish to thank the editorial and production teams at Corwin Press, whose skills and assistance were essential to this volume.

Special thanks from the author and Corwin Press to the following individuals whose suggestions and thoughtful critiques helped hone this book:

Jackie Colbert
Assistant Director
Division of School
   Improvement
North Carolina Department of
   Public Instruction
Raleigh, NC

John Eller
Assistant Professor/Corwin
   Author
Educational Development and
   Leadership
Southwest Minnesota
   State University
Marshall, MN

Sue Elliott
Former President
Staff Development Council of
   British Columbia
West Vancouver, BC

Gwen E. Gross
Superintendent
Manhattan Beach Unified
   School District
Manhattan Beach, CA

Jim Hoogheem
Principal
Fernbrook Elementary School
Maple Grove, MN

Susan Hudson
Former President
Tennessee Staff Development
  Council
Nashville, TN

Kathleen O'Neill
Director
Leadership Professional
  Initiative
Atlanta, GA

Karla Reiss
Former President
New York State Staff
  Development Council
New Rochelle, NY

Dennis Sparks
Executive Director/Corwin
  Author
National Staff Development
  Council
Ann Arbor, MI

Paul Young
Principal/Corwin Author
West Elementary School
Lancaster, OH

About the Author

 **Marilyn Tallerico** is a professor of Educational Leadership at Syracuse University. She teaches graduate courses in professional development, curriculum leadership, assessment of teaching, and politics of education. Her work has appeared in the *Journal of Staff Development,* as well as numerous other research and practitioner journals. She is widely published in the areas of the superintendency, gender, and educational leadership. Her two prior books were *City Schools: Leading the Way* (1993) and *Accessing the Superintendency: The Unwritten Rules* (2000), the former coedited with Patrick B. Forsyth.

A theme throughout her work is how educational leaders can promote equity and excellence in the public schools. She has facilitated professional development for school board members, administrators, and teachers. She currently serves on the editorial board of the *American Educational Research Journal* and has previously served on the boards of *The Educational Administration Quarterly* and the *Journal of School Leadership.* Her community service and scholarship have been supported by the Educational Foundation of the American Association of University Women, the National Policy Board on Educational Administration, and the New York State Association for Women in Administration.

Prior to her position at the university, Marilyn served 12 years in the public schools in Connecticut and Arizona. She has been a central office curriculum administrator, a coordinator of bilingual and English-as-a-Second-Language programs, and a Spanish teacher.

Marilyn earned her PhD in Educational Leadership and Policy Studies at Arizona State University and her master's and undergraduate degrees at the University of Connecticut. In addition to her professional interests, she is an avid outdoors person, a happy kayaker, and a hopeful golfer.

PART I

Determining Content

1

How Should Adult and Student Learning Be Linked?

A collective groan can be heard as you finish distributing the three-page questionnaire during the afterschool faculty meeting. Undaunted, you enthusiastically urge the staff, "Please respond to each item on this Needs Assessment, as it will help the School Improvement Committee plan our professional development program for the year." The sixth-grade team leader raises her hand to ask, "What do you think they mean by 'some' on the degree-of-interest scale from 'none' to 'much'?" Another teacher observes, "It seems like we just filled out one of these for the science grant application we submitted last month." The Reading Specialist clarifies, "No, I think that was the staff survey required for the accreditation review."

Do the teachers you work with have similar concerns about surveys and rankings of their interests, perceptions, or preferences? What are some alternatives to the paper-and-pencil needs assessments that frequently accompany school improvement planning? Are there better ways to determine what the focus of your school's adult learning initiatives should be?

This chapter addresses these and other questions important to decision making about worthwhile professional development *content.* In the past, questionnaires such as the one alluded to in the opening vignette were often relied upon for identifying the content, substance, or topics for teachers' continuing education on the job. But state-of-the-art thinking about professional development content has shifted in recent years. As this chapter describes and illustrates those shifts, there are three key points to keep in mind:

1. Student learning priorities should drive adult learning content.

2. Micro- and macro-level student needs' analysis can help define priorities.

3. Data analysis can be simplified.

Why the Shift Away From Adult Needs Assessment?

There are several reasons why written surveys of teachers' needs have fallen out of favor as the preferred means of targeting professional development content. First, it is debatable whether the results of such assessments more accurately reflect respondents' needs rather than wants. In part, the concern is that sometimes what we want is not really what we need. Additionally, even when framed anonymously, experienced professionals may be reluctant to identify genuine areas of weakness, uncertainty, or needs that warrant improvement or intervention. On both these counts, the validity of the data derived from adult needs assessment is called into question.

Second, constructivist and democratic theories of teaching, learning, and curriculum improvement have garnered renewed attention in recent years (Beane, 2002; Brooks & Brooks, 1999). These perspectives converge around the idea of increasing student-centeredness. Applying this idea involves developing creative responses to questions such as: How can I more actively engage all children in today's language arts lessons? How can we design school experiences so that students help each other learn? And how can we construct curricula that build on today's youths' interests? Extrapolating learner-centered, constructivist themes to teachers' professional development means making students' (rather than adults') needs the primary, substantive focus.

Third, education's current political environment emphasizes students' learning *outcomes,* often as measured by performance on standards-driven exams. Consistent with this emphasis, the value of children's test results and other forms of student data has been elevated significantly in recent years. That value is reinforced in expert opinion about best practices for professional development (Holloway, J., 2003; Killion, 2002; Lindstrom & Speck, 2004; National Staff Development Council, 2001; Sparks, 2002). That is, the content of teachers' on-the-job continuing education should be derived from data on student learning needs—not the needs of adults who may respond to a survey questionnaire about their interests or preferences.

There will always be times when formal, written assessments of teachers' thinking, observations, knowledge, and practice are useful (e.g., school climate surveys and program evaluations of various sorts, including those described in Chapter 2). Currently, however, two other approaches to determining the content of professional development are considered more student-centered and, therefore, more meaningful. One is guided by a micro-level perspective and is strongly curriculum-based. The other emphasizes macro-level data-based decision-making processes. Familiarity with both approaches will strengthen your repertoire of strategies for linking the content of adult professional development to students' learning needs.

Micro-Level Strategies for Focusing on Students' Needs

What should be the content of teachers' professional development? From a micro-level perspective, the answer is short and straightforward: *the curriculum.* More specifically, the parts of the curriculum that students are struggling with most.

In this context, the curriculum means the lessons, units, assignments, and instruction students routinely experience. The curriculum also includes the projects, performances, products, and tests through which their learning is assessed on a regular basis. The focus is on what children experience every day in classrooms—the taught and tested curriculum.

In today's schools, of course, district and state standards shape the curriculum that children in a particular grade or subject area experience. Standards for what students should know and be able to do also serve as common reference points around which teachers can identify student underperformance and other learning needs.

So, what would the adults in your school be doing if their professional development centered on the parts of the everyday curriculum that students were struggling with most? Several things.

Everyday Lessons

Sometimes, they would be meeting in grade-level, content area, or other relevant teams to share, discuss, develop, revise, monitor, and problem-solve around what they teach in common. For groups with solid working relationships and team leaders, potentially productive discussion starters might sound as informal as the following questions.

Discussion Starters

- Here are examples I've used to illustrate "X" concept or skill. What are others you've found helpful for students who have difficulty "getting it" the first time around?
- We'll all be including a unit on "Y" at some point this quarter. How are you thinking about your plans? And what might we learn from the last time some of our students didn't achieve mastery on this standard?
- I was disappointed with the essays I received when I assigned "Z." Could the group take a look at both my instructions for the task and my lower-performing students' essays to come up with suggestions for how it might be possible to get better results next time?
- The two new members of our team haven't yet taught "ABC." How can we help them anticipate the misconceptions students will likely come with, the questions that will arise, and the trouble spots students typically encounter?

What these conversation prompts have in common is: (a) their focus on a particular skill, idea, or standard students are having difficulty with; (b) their reliance on teachers' formative assessments and direct observations of students' struggles; and (c) the intent to modify strategies by drawing on other teachers' insights. (See Chapter 3 for more on Collaborative Problem Solving and Action Research as two of five possible design options for professional development.) Thus, the *content* for adult learning is clear and targeted to the near term: one lesson or strategy at a time from the curriculum students experience every day (Schmoker, 2004).

Setting a measurable goal for the selected skill or underachieved standard can help focus content even more sharply (Killion, 2002). Schmoker (2002) shares the example of a team of teachers concerned that just 4 of 90 children were succeeding with writing "descriptive settings," a particular kind of narrative assessed through a rubric used in their state. The teachers studied exemplars available in curriculum guidebooks and brainstormed alternative ways of teaching descriptive settings. They collectively developed a new lesson they each would use in their classrooms before evaluating students' writing again and meeting a month later. The results were that 85 of the 90 students wrote better descriptive settings when assessed with the same rubric after the targeted intervention. Change experts point out that small steps and tangible classroom results such as these can motivate teachers and impact student performance more directly than larger, more complex, school improvement initiatives typically do (Fullan, 2000).

Teacher-Made Assessments

The foregoing examples focused primarily on teachers' monitoring, adjusting, and refining particular *lessons*. A slightly different approach to centering adult learning on students' everyday classroom experience involves teachers creating and administering common *assessments* (Schmoker, 2003). That is, adult teams collectively develop and examine the results of unit quizzes, tests, or other performance assessments that all children take regardless of who is teaching the course or grade-level section. In order to do this, teachers must inevitably grapple with the standards, skills, and knowledge most important for students to learn, as well as what students should be expected to show as evidence of that learning. Team scrutiny of student outcomes on these teacher-made assessments can then prompt idea sharing and working together to improve upon common student weaknesses (DuFour, 2002a).

Student Work

In addition to everyday lessons and common assessments, a third source of adult learning content centered on children's needs is the actual work that students create. It can take myriad forms, including written responses to problems they are asked to solve, science lab results, videotapes of presentations they make, exhibits they produce, projects they complete, writing samples, portfolios in various subject areas, or any other products resulting from assignments and class activities.

Similar to the lessons and assessments mentioned earlier, these work samples become the focus of teacher discussion and problem solving around how to improve student performance (Langer, Colter, & Goff, 2003; Roberts & Pruitt, 2003). As such, student work related to the standards and learning goals considered essential for a particular grade level or subject area may be the best kind of example to start with. Initial questions for group deliberation might include: What essential skills and knowledge does this work sample demonstrate? What weaknesses or gaps in knowledge does it illustrate? What evidence of ability to synthesize information appears in this sample? What do these samples suggest students are struggling with most?

Although all of the previous questions focus exclusively on the students' work, connections to curriculum and instruction logically follow. What are some ways the teacher's prompts can bring out higher-level thinking? How could the assignment be altered to inspire greater student creativity? What additional supports does this child evidently need? How might we change the course syllabus to address the recurring weaknesses that appear in these samples?

Guides That Can Help

Clearly, not all grade-level or subject area teachers will have experience productively discussing student work or developing common lessons and assessments. Nor will all groups have a history of fruitful problem solving around student underperformance. In these cases, experienced group facilitators and more structured processes for focusing curricular dialogues will be required (Richardson, 2001a). Chapter 3 provides a broad overview of Collaborative Problem Solving and Action Research as two of five design options for professional development. However, you should also be aware that numerous protocols (discussion guides) for examining student work and studying lessons together are available online. You can quickly access many practical, ready-to-use tools developed by the Annenberg Institute for School Reform (www.lasw.org) and the Coalition of Essential Schools (www.essentialschools.org).

What many of these protocols have in common are guiding questions to help group members stay focused on describing and improving the work (rather than judging it or nitpicking). They often also specify sequences of procedures so as to ensure active listening and turn taking to better capitalize on all members' insights. All are aimed at clarifying and deepening teachers' reflection on, and constructive problem solving around, issues important to student learning.

Curriculum-Based Adult Learning Content

The three foci for adult learning reviewed thus far—lessons, assessments, and student work—all are intended to keep professional development content grounded in the classroom. They share an emphasis on teachers collaborating to decrease children's struggles with the curriculum routinely experienced in a particular grade or subject area. They are guided by a micro-level perspective on what is most important for continuous professional growth: improving one lesson, assignment, or assessment at a time. This perspective serves as a valuable lens for understanding and supporting adult development.

But savvy school leaders view their organizations from multiple vantage points, using a variety of lenses. Accordingly, I turn next to a more systemic, macro-level perspective for determining what the content of teachers' professional development should be. It too is aimed at linking adult learning to students' learning needs. However, it is based on: (a) more varied sources of student data, (b) more systematic analysis of those data, (c) patterns of needs beyond individual classrooms, and (d) schoolwide priorities (Killion, 2002).

A Macro-Level Strategy for Focusing on Students' Needs

From a whole-school perspective, what are some examples of the range of student data from which foci for adult professional development can be derived?

- Grades earned
- Affective or attitudinal assessment (e.g., report card commentary on effort, interests, cooperation, motivation, etc.)
- Attendance records
- Participation in extracurricular activities or community service
- Graduation and dropout rates
- College attendance or postsecondary employment information
- Homework completion rates

- Enrollments in special education, remedial, gifted and talented, advanced placement, honors, and other targeted programs
- Disciplinary referrals, detentions, suspensions, and expulsions
- Portfolios, writing rubrics, and other project-based or performance assessment results
- Teacher-made test results
- Standardized or other test scores
- Socioeconomic status (e.g., poverty indicators such as eligibility for free or reduced price lunch)
- Demographics (e.g., race, ethnicity, sex, English language proficiency)

Strategies for Success

There are several features of this sample listing that suggest practical action steps for school leaders:

1. Capitalize on existing data before taking the time and trouble to gather more. If your school is like most in the United States, you are already required to gather, tally, and periodically report (to your community, district office, or state education department) on many of the items listed earlier. Also, virtually every time your school or a collaborating agency submits a grant or other funding request, careful documentation of pressing needs is included. Avoid duplication of effort by taking advantage of all such existing data about your students.

2. Focus on information most important to your school's mission and unique context. In some communities in recent years, there has been a backlash against overreliance on high-stakes testing and other single measures of student achievement. You will notice that the examples listed above purposefully span a wide range of academic, affective, and demographic indicators. Because individual schools' visions reflect differences in student outcomes most highly valued, improvement efforts (including those aimed at teachers' professional development) should be aligned with those values. For example, if creating well-rounded, contributing citizens is the school's most valued outcome, then participation rates in extracurricular activities and community service may be the data warranting considerable attention. In contrast, if admission to college is the top priority, then grades earned and SAT data may be the more appropriate foci. Because you will not be able to give equal attention to all data, being selective—and consistent with the local school community's values—is key.

3. Rely on longitudinal data whenever possible. Just as multiple sources of data are preferable to single sources, multiyear data can almost always provide a more complete picture of your students than data for a single point in time. Virtually all of the variables bulleted earlier are or could be collected over several years. Longitudinal data have the potential to more clearly illustrate patterns. They enable analysis of trends and serve as a check on intermittent blips in data. Because school improvement efforts (and their associated professional development) will be more effective if sustained over time (Fullan, 2000; Gordon, 2004; Sparks, 2002), you will want your interventions to be aimed at the most enduring challenges.

Gap Analysis

Let's assume you have taken these three principles to heart and are ready to work with these or other selected student data. What is it you should be looking for in the data? The short answer is *gaps,* that is, differences or discrepancies between where your students—or some identifiable subset of them—currently are and where you and your school community would like them to be.

How to get from the data to the gaps? Analysis. More specifically, through one of two general approaches to analysis as follows:

a. *Detailed,* methodologically rigorous, statistical, or qualitative content analysis. Choose this option if your central office, regional service center, or state education department has the staff, expertise, and other resources needed to conduct comprehensive reviews of your data at a reasonable cost and time schedule. This option may also be feasible if there are able and willing colleges, universities, or doctoral dissertation students at your school's disposal.
b. *Simplified,* statistically imperfect but potentially telling gap analysis. Choose this option if you and your school teams will need to work with the data yourselves. The remainder of this chapter is devoted to this, rather than the first, approach.

Simplifying Data Analysis

For our purposes here, it helps to think of the key, component activities of gap analysis in terms of the following (see Figure 1.1):

- Careful examination
- Sorting

Figure 1.1   Gap Analysis Model

Following these steps can help link adult professional development content to students' most important learning needs.

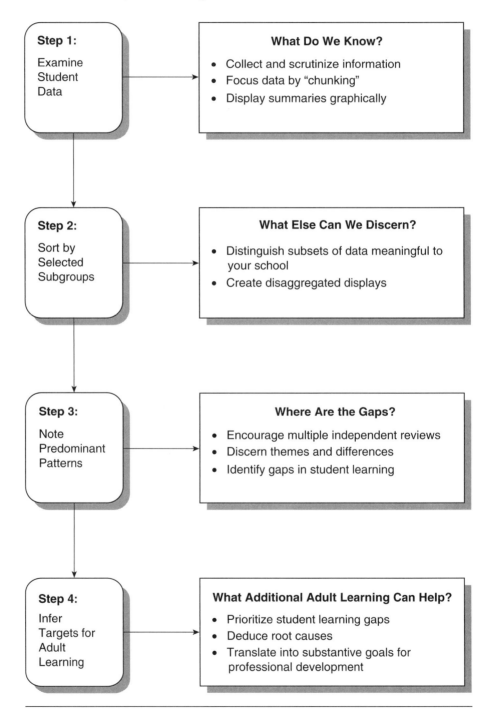

- Pattern recognition
- Making inferences

Why these terms? First, they represent skills and abilities you and your colleagues already have. This language frames analysis as a series of doable and manageable (rather than formidable or onerous) tasks. Second, these are also competencies teachers often work at cultivating in their students and, thus, can easily relate to. What does each entail?

Careful Examination

Study and scrutiny are helpful synonyms here. Commonplace study tools are applicable. For example, begin by reading and rereading the data, then *chunk* it into more compressed forms. In the case of numbers, chunking typically means tallying, calculating averages, and converting tallies into percentages. For qualitative (word-based) information, it involves grouping similar data into categories. Chunking also means displaying in formats that lend themselves to accessible, visual examination, such as graphs, tables, outlines, or concept maps (Killion, 2002). The figures and tables interspersed throughout this book are examples of useful summary display formats.

Sample questions to guide data examination might include: What have been the commonly recurring reasons for our students' absences? Which elements of the writing rubric do students appear to have mastered? Which elements have they not? What have been our students' average scores on the statewide third- and eighth-grade tests in language arts and mathematics? On which subtests of those disciplines are our students performing best? Worst? Which items on the exams are our students most frequently answering correctly? Incorrectly?

Sorting

The synonym you may frequently hear today is *disaggregation*. For example, the No Child Left Behind Act of 2001 requires that student achievement exam data be sorted and reported (that is, disaggregated) by specific subgroups: students receiving special education services, students who are English language learners, students identified by race, and students in numerous other categories. Your own school community's priorities and values may suggest other relevant subsets warranting disaggregation.

Sorting by category typically involves asking more focused questions of the data, as well as chunking and comparing them in different ways. For example, What has been our female students' rate of participation in advanced mathematics and science courses? How does this rate compare to the males' rate? On which subtests of the fifth-grade social studies exams have our Hispanic students been doing best? Worst? How do those strengths and weaknesses compare to the performance of our Caucasian students? The demographic and socioeconomic data you collect about your students will make this kind of sorting possible.

Pattern Recognition

The graphs, charts, and other kinds of summary displays suggested earlier can help make apparent any regularities or variations (that is, patterns) in your students' data. Patterns may include qualitative characteristics, quantifiable increases or decreases over time, identification of anomalies or outliers, similarities and differences among subgroups, and other kinds of recurring themes or changes. Some patterns may reveal small differences that affect many students. Others may be large differences that affect relatively small numbers of students. Either pattern can signal important areas warranting attention and intervention.

As anyone who has ever taken a Rorschach test can confirm, the same inkblot will suggest quite different things to different people. Similarly, as individual teachers, administrators, or community members, we may notice different patterns in the same data display or set of information. To enrich your analysis by taking advantage of these potentially diverse insights, ask a variety of people to independently review the same data summaries, sorts, and graphic representations (Killion, 2002). The key questions to ask are: What, if any, patterns do you see? Which patterns suggest gaps between where our students currently are and where we would like them to be?

Making Inferences

This final stage of the process demands considerable professional judgment and negotiation, to translate gap analyses into actionable next steps. More specifically, it involves interpreting salient patterns and reaching consensus in the following three key areas:

1. Which gaps in student learning are the most important to us as a school? This question recognizes that most schools will have more gaps than resources to address all of them well. Therefore, student needs will have to be prioritized so that improvement efforts can be targeted and the finite resources available can be brought to bear most effectively.

2. *What do we think are causing these results?* This second question underscores the importance of root cause analysis—of thinking carefully and creatively to discern what may really lie beneath students' less-than-desirable performance. There will likely be multiple factors contributing to significant gaps in student learning (Killion, 2002; McTighe & Thomas, 2003). For example, some factors may relate directly to the curriculum: Is there a mismatch between what is tested in second-grade arithmetic and our school's curriculum goals for that grade? Some factors may center on instructional materials: How does the biology textbook we adopted address the gap we have identified in our students' science knowledge? Some factors will point to the students themselves: Are our poorest essay writers the adolescents who have the worst attendance in the middle grades? Then what is at the root of many of their absences? Some contributors may relate directly to school structures and programs: Are support systems available in time to intervene and remediate early difficulties in reading? Some contributors to key gaps may have to do with district policies: How, if at all, does the new zero-tolerance policy for fighting relate to at-risk students' falling further behind? And some factors will relate more directly to the adult staff's current knowledge and skills: How familiar are our teachers with varied instructional strategies that foster the kinds of student problem solving required on today's state exams? Accordingly, your overall school improvement planning will likely involve several categories for action, including, perhaps, curriculum development, materials acquisition, academic assistance programming, community partnerships, and policy revision. Adult professional development is but one of a number of possible interventions.

Just as it was necessary to prioritize student learning gaps judged most important to you as a school, the results of root cause analyses will likely also require ranking and prioritizing, in order to be able to effectively target next steps. It will always be better for your school to focus its improvement efforts on addressing the most salient root causes in-depth and well, rather than to create numerous interventions that scatter resources among all possible contributing factors. The latter leads to fragmentation and overload, rather than sustainable change that can make a difference to students (Fullan, 2001).

3. Of the root causes our school can do something about, what goals for adult learning can help us narrow the gap(s)? This question recognizes that there will be some contributing factors that your school can ameliorate and others that are beyond its current capacity. It also reinforces several premises that will resurface throughout this book. First, supporting teachers' continuous development on the job is an important piece of comprehensive school improvement (Gordon, 2004). Second, goals for adult learning should be specified both to make clear its purpose and to enable evaluation of effectiveness (Guskey, 2000; Killion, 2002). Third and most important, top-priority student needs should drive the goals and determine the content for adult learning (Holloway, J., 2003; Killion, 2002).

What does inferring professional development targets from student learning gaps look like in practice? Let's say your analysis of data across four different subject areas at the middle school reveals high performance on fact-based comprehension, but recurring and widespread poor performance on items requiring the application of knowledge in new situations. A general staff development goal might be for teachers to implement four different instructional strategies that have been shown to improve adolescents' abilities to *use* (rather than simply recall) concepts. A more specific goal might be that, in the marking period following their completion of relevant forms of professional development geared to the four strategies, teachers will share two lessons they have created that demonstrate their use of two of the four strategies requiring students to apply previous knowledge to a new problem. A follow-up goal might be that, after receiving feedback on the lessons and participating in peer coaching, teachers will share with others in their department at least five student work samples representing assignments based on the teacher's implementation of three of the strategies learned. A capstone goal might require teachers to share examples of student work that demonstrate improvement in students' abilities to apply selected knowledge or concepts to new situations.

This progression of goals suggests that staff development targets should shift from adult learning to student outcomes, as time and supports for teacher development increase. Additionally, as Chapter 2 will underscore, the more specific and measurable the adult learning goal, the more useful it is to assessing which professional development initiatives have been successful and which may warrant revision.

An Image of Success

The Director of Curriculum and Instruction has been facilitating afterschool meetings with your faculty for about eight weeks. She has guided the staff through a methodical process of analyzing student data to identify significant gaps in learning. Although initially disconcerted by the range of student underperformance, the Director's adept facilitation helped you and your teachers reach a decision about what to target.

Improving students' reading comprehension became a top priority. Three related goals for teachers' professional development were generated, each emphasizing instructional strategies for increasing reading comprehension across subject areas.

School Improvement Committee members took the lead on investigating relevant resources. They examined research studies, instructional materials, and Web sites. They contacted several expert consultants and schools where reading comprehension gains were impressive. Their investigations included tough questions, such as: What do best practices for improving comprehension look like? Where have they been implemented? Under what conditions? With what resources? (Killion, 2002).

The particular formats for your school's adult professional development have yet to be determined, but its substantive focus is now clear. Most teachers are pleased to have an unambiguous direction for the school's collective efforts.

Summary

Gone are the days when the most renowned school district staff development programs were the ones with the heftiest, most comprehensive catalogs of topics from which teachers selected their preferred focus. This chapter has described and illustrated two more student-centered means of determining what the *content* for your schools' adult learning initiatives should be:

- A big picture, schoolwide data analysis strategy that situates teachers' professional development among other school improvement priorities
- A smaller scale, curriculum-driven process aimed at improving one lesson, assessment, or student product at a time, within particular grade levels and subject areas

Both approaches rely on you and your teams accomplishing the following tasks:

1. Identifying gaps in student learning

2. Deriving adult learning targets from those student needs

Moreover, both approaches share many of the features of the backward design procedures you and your teachers have grown accustomed to using for curriculum development and revision (McTighe & Thomas, 2003; Wiggins & McTighe, 1998). That is, starting with the end in mind, set specific goals or standards for student learning (Killion, 2002).

Next Steps

Now that the focus of your school's professional development has been clarified, you need to devise a plan for tracking progress toward targets for adult and student growth. In the next chapter, additional strategies are suggested to help guide the longer-term implementation of the content you and your faculty have decided upon.

2

How Can Professional Development Be Evaluated?

> *The gap analysis process at your school has consumed considerable time and energy. You share your teachers' sense of accomplishment for having agreed upon clear content targets. In the past, the school's staff development had tended to veer from one topic to another. You feel fortunate that the district's Curriculum Director was willing to facilitate the school's data analysis, prioritizing, and professional development goal setting. You are pleased with the thoroughness of the School Improvement Committee's research on reading comprehension strategies appropriate for diverse subject areas.*
>
> *It is now the Director's final meeting with teachers. Just as you rise to celebrate closure on focusing content and to publicly thank the Director, she continues animatedly, "Now let's move on to think about evaluation, so you can complete your professional development planning."*

W hy fuss about evaluating staff development before it has even begun? Doesn't evaluation typically come at the end of a set of activities or program? Aren't there more important things to attend to at the start of your school's professional development initiatives? And wasn't the first part of this book to be centered on best practices for determining adult learning *content*? How does evaluation relate to content?

This chapter will address these questions by explaining and illustrating an evaluation process useful for teachers' professional development. Most of the chapter's information is derived from the early work of training expert Donald Kirkpatrick (1959, 1977, 1998), as subsequently expanded and adapted to education by Thomas Guskey (2000) and Joellen Killion (2002).

What school leaders most need to understand about these issues are the following:

1. Evaluation planning complements gap analyses.

2. Both focus on desired student learning outcomes.

3. Professional development evaluation can be simplified to five interrelated tiers of questioning.

Evaluation as Content

As emphasized in the previous chapter, specific goals and priorities for student learning should drive the content of your school's adult learning initiatives—for example, increasing the number of sixth-grade students whose persuasive essays earn proficient ratings on the writing rubric common to the middle school; decreasing the proportion of African American students placed in remedial math resource rooms at the high school; or, similar to the previous vignettes, improving children's reading comprehension as determined by some agreed-upon assessments in the classroom.

Stating student learning priorities in concrete and measurable terms provides clear targets for collective improvement efforts of all sorts. Such statements can represent what you and your school have decided are worthwhile, feasible ends to work toward together over a particular time period. They can also serve as standards against which the progress of efforts can be assessed—that is, as evaluative criteria (Killion, 2002).

In this way, evaluation planning functions as a second and complementary means of determining the content for adult professional development. Similar to the gap analyses described in Chapter 1, the identification of evaluation criteria in terms of children's learning outcomes is a student-centered means of focusing the substance of adult learning by "beginning with the end in mind" (Covey, 1989, p. 3). What, more specifically, does that look and sound like in practice?

Working Backward

Although professional development experts agree on the importance of knowing what you are looking to achieve before beginning, they also acknowledge the challenges and complexity of improving student learning (Killion, 2002). To make that complexity more manageable, Guskey (2000) recommends thinking of evaluation in terms of five interdependent levels or stages of questioning. The five levels are numbered in the chronological order in which they would proceed in time; that is, with Level 1 occurring first, Level 2 second, and so on. However, working backward from the highest level is a way of breaking down the ultimate goal of increased student learning into a series of smaller, more practicable steps for professional development planning (Guskey, 2002).

The five levels of assessment, as applied to teachers' professional development, are the following:

- Level 1: Teachers' reactions
- Level 2: Teachers' learning
- Level 3: Organizational support and change
- Level 4: Teachers' use of new knowledge and skills
- Level 5: Student learning outcomes

Table 2.1 (see p. 22) illustrates how the chronological sequence for *conducting* a multitiered evaluation is reversed for *planning* purposes.

The remainder of this chapter elaborates each level of questioning in planning backward.

Student Learning Outcomes: Level 5

The more explicit you are about what the top-priority gaps in student learning are, the more focused your goals for improved learning outcomes can be. Accordingly, the questions to be asked at this level of assessment will be quite particular to your school. They will be as varied as the goals you and your teachers have targeted for

Table 2.1   Evaluating Professional Development Using Five Levels

Chronological sequence for conducting evaluation	*Suggested sequence for planning evaluation backward*
1) Teachers' reactions	5) Student learning outcomes
2) Teachers' learning	4) Teachers' use of new knowledge and skills
3) Organizational support	3) Organizational support
4) Teachers' use of new knowledge and skills	2) Teachers' learning
5) Student learning outcomes	1) Teachers' reactions

SOURCE: Adapted from Guskey (2000). Thomas R. Guskey, *Evaluating professional development*, pp. 79–81, copyright 2000 by Corwin Press. Reprinted by permission of Corwin Press, Inc.

students. For example, evaluating professional development initiatives at Level 5 could mean asking questions such as:

- Has students' reading comprehension improved?
- Are children writing more coherent paragraphs now than they were before?
- Is the dropout rate for sophomores decreasing?
- In what ways are students demonstrating higher-level thinking?
- How, if at all, were children's attitudes affected?

These examples represent minor variations on the questions suggested previously for examining existing school data to identify discrepancies between where your students currently are and where you would like them to be (Killion, 2002). Often, the key difference is that, for assessing progress toward goals, questions will be stated in ways that reflect the direction of desired improvement (e.g., truancy going down; test scores going up). However, more open-ended questions aimed at qualitative changes may be equally important to you and your school. For example, "How, if at all, have students' contributions to class discussions changed?" Again, the assessment queries will depend on your goals for student learning.

Substantiating Movement Toward Goals

What sources will you and your school community trust as indicators of these ups, downs, or other more open-ended qualities? This is a critical issue to grapple with at the same time that questions for assessing student learning targets are identified (Guskey, 2002, 2003b; Killion, 2002). Options to consider (and to specify up front) are: student work samples, portfolios, grades, scores on particular tests, projects of particular kinds, student interviews, parent surveys, or other school, teacher, or student records.

A key leadership task is to elicit staff consensus that the agreed-upon sources are reasonable and credible indicators of desired student learning outcomes. Can we agree, for example, that the results of the bimonthly quizzes accompanying the school's reading textbook series will be the measure we will use for gauging movement toward reading comprehension goals? What are the two or three things we will be looking for in samples of sixth-grade students' writing that will tell us their paragraphs exhibit coherence? Will we accept teacher reports of student attitude change, or do we need to enlist the local university's student teachers to record observations of children in classrooms?

You and your teams may simply want to use the same data sources that helped surface the student learning gap(s) in the first place. Or additional, more frequent, or alternative indicators and checkpoints toward goals may be warranted.

Teachers' Use of New Knowledge and Skills: Level 4

Continuing on the planning path backward from targeted student outcomes, this level centers on the *instructional practices* shown to help children attain the knowledge, skills, or dispositions identified as priority learning goals. As suggested in Chapter 1, you and your school have already determined what the substantive focus for teachers' professional development will be, based on salient student learning gaps. For example, because of recurring student reading comprehension difficulties, goals for teachers' professional development center on learning or refining instructional strategies for increasing reading comprehension across subject areas. Hence, relevant evaluation questions at this level might be the following:

- How frequently are teachers using these new reading comprehension strategies in their classrooms?

- How well are teachers implementing the strategies?
- Are teachers applying the knowledge or skills that were the focus of our schools' professional development initiatives?
- If so, which elements are they consistently using as intended?
- Which elements appear to warrant additional support, practice, or time to master?

Answers to questions such as these serve several important purposes. First, they can help reshape the content of ongoing and future professional development efforts. For example, if your original content focus included five distinct instructional strategies, and most teachers appear to be implementing two of them proficiently, then it may be helpful to focus subsequent adult learning opportunities on one or more of the three other strategies. Or, it might be appropriate to determine why teachers do not find some of the suggested strategies useful and, again, readjust future opportunities based on that feedback.

Another purpose evaluation at Level 4 serves is to monitor the improvement initiatives put into place in the classroom to help meet student learning targets. Remember that you originally selected adult learning goals related to root causes you and your teachers believed you could impact. Honing teaching practices, alone, will not suffice. (See the ensuing discussion of Level 3 for additional environmental factors contributing to student learning.) However, it is important to assess whether and how agreed-upon changes in instructional practices are being enacted. This is the essence of evaluation at Level 4.

Again, school leaders must also raise the question of what will be trusted as evidence that teachers are using the new skills or applying the new knowledge in their classrooms. And, as before, the time to answer that question is up front, when the substance of teachers' learning is being determined. Guskey (2002) suggests a number of sources of potentially trustworthy information, including the following:

- Asking teachers to self-report, through interviews, group discussions, or questionnaires
- Examining teaching portfolios
- Reading teachers' written reflections
- Reviewing audio- or videotapes of instruction
- Observing directly in classrooms

Observations can be focused, for example, on reading comprehension teaching and learning strategies, both as follow-up to initial schoolwide professional development and to gain a sense of how widely and well teachers are implementing particular instructional approaches. Several authors recommend means of classroom observations other than conventional visits by individual administrators or teacher colleagues. Examples of such alternatives include the following:

- Brief *walk-throughs* of multiple classrooms by teams of teachers and administrators to sample broadly and create a composite schoolwide portrait (Richardson, 2001b)
- Lengthier *data-in-a-day* self-study processes that can include students and teachers elected by their peers, also visiting numerous classrooms in teams to note the presence or absence of agreed-upon teaching and learning strategies (Walsh, Sattes, & Wiman, 2001)

Whether through self-report, observation, or other forms of information gathering, the purpose of assessment at Level 4 is to gauge the school's—rather than any one teacher's—progress at putting its professional development goals into practice in classrooms.

Organizational Support and Change: Level 3

Supportive policies, strong leadership, sufficient resources, and positive climate are also integral to the success of instructional and curricular changes aimed at increasing student learning (Newmann, Smith, Allensworth, & Bryk, 2001). Accordingly, they too should be a part of evaluating professional development. Examples of questions to address at this level are the following:

- How much time and follow-up are provided to help teachers implement new reading comprehension strategies?
- Are appropriate materials available to teachers and students?
- Are structures in place that allow staff to collaborate regularly?
- Does the school culture value experimentation and risk taking in the classroom?
- How do leaders recognize and celebrate initial successes on the way to school improvement targets?
- How congruent are school policies and practices with professional development content?

These kinds of questions underscore the interdependent relationship between organizational context and improvement goals. They also illustrate how professional development can be either supported or thwarted by broader organizational factors. Guskey (2002) offers the example of how a school's professional development focus on increasing cooperative learning approaches and team projects in classrooms can be undermined by schoolwide grading and recognition practices that exclusively reward individual, rather than collaborative, performance.

Chapters 5 through 7 will provide other examples, principles, and strategies for creating contexts that help, rather than hinder, students' and teachers' learning in schools. The point here, however, is that, because these organizational contextual variables are so powerful, they need to be a part of both planning and assessing adult professional development.

Again, knowing what you are looking for before beginning is essential to specifying the evidence you and your school will trust as indicators of organizational support. The following are potential sources of information:

- District and school records of funding and duration of professional development initiatives
- Teacher interviews or questionnaires about the quality and frequency of support for improvement efforts
- School climate surveys
- Reviews of administrators' portfolios or reflections on practice
- District administrators' observations and evaluations of school-based leadership
- Policy reviews aimed at discerning (in)consistencies with professional development goals

Teachers' Learning: Level 2

So far, the recommended tiers of evaluation questioning have involved indicators of: (a) children's learning, (b) teachers' use of new knowledge and skills in the classroom, and (c) organizational support for (a) and (b). Continuing on a path backward from targeted student outcomes, this level of assessment centers on what teachers learned from the professional development experience (Guskey, 2002). Whereas Level 4 questions seek to determine whether teachers are able to *use* what they learned, Level 2 aims more simply to assess the *acquisition* of new knowledge or skills. This distinction can also be understood as knowing something in the abstract (Level 2), versus being able to transfer and apply what was learned to classroom practice (Level 4).

Evaluating professional development initiatives at Level 2 might involve asking questions such as the following:

- What proportion of elementary teachers can describe five different techniques for improving students' reading comprehension?
- Can teachers identify which reading comprehension strategy a sample written lesson plan illustrates?
- Can they develop a unit of their own that relies on at least two of the five strategies?
- How many teachers can pass a brief quiz on the content of their professional development?
- Which elements require additional learning?

Information gained through questions such as these can help reshape the content of ongoing and future professional development efforts. Equally important, if assessment results at this level suggest that large numbers of teachers have not yet fully understood the intended content, then it would be unrealistic to expect application or use with students in their classrooms. The latter are higher-level skills requiring solid foundational knowledge. Level 2 assessments of professional development are geared to ascertaining the quality of that foundation.

Possible sources of such information include the following:

- Traditional paper-and-pencil quizzes or tests
- Review of teachers' written plans, reflections, or portfolios
- Teachers' demonstrations or simulations in the professional development practice environment

As suggested for each of Guskey's (2000) five levels, teachers and administrators should jointly determine the kinds of indicators that will be feasible and trusted as evidence of the adult learning expected from professional development initiatives. Moreover, those agreements should be arrived at simultaneous to planning content (Killion, 2002).

Teachers' Reactions: Level 1

Historically, staff development evaluation focused exclusively on teacher reactions. This assessment level is aimed at determining participants' satisfaction with the professional development experience. In contrast to Level 2's focus on "Did we *get* it?," Level 1 is primarily concerned with "Did we *like* it?"

You are probably already quite familiar with the kinds of questions characterizing this level of evaluation (Guskey, 2002):

- Was the information on reading comprehension strategies interesting?
- How knowledgeable was the facilitator?
- Were the materials provided helpful?
- What did you think of this format for professional development?
- What changes would you recommend for the future?
- How would you grade this learning experience overall?

Simple written rating scales and questionnaires, or interviews with individuals or groups can be used to gather such impressions. Questions may range from highly structured to completely open-ended, as illustrated by the preceding bulleted examples.

Participant feedback at this level can help you and your teams modify both the content and design of subsequent professional development opportunities. (See Chapter 3 for more on design.) When assessment is limited to this tier of questioning, it tends to keep the focus on adults' needs and perceptions, rather than student learning priorities. In tandem with the other four levels of assessment, however, attention to adult participants' reactions can help move professional development toward student-centered goals. See Figure 2.1 for a sample evaluation plan that includes key questions at all five levels.

Why Is Evaluating Professional Development Important?

Taken together we see the following:

- Teachers' affective reactions to development experiences
- Their cognitive learning from those experiences
- Their application of that learning in interactions with students
- The school's systemic supports for adults' and children's growth

All these represent key within-school contributors to (or detractors from) students' learning. Each of these elements must be working in harmony and well, to help bring about desired student outcomes. Additionally, breakdowns at any one of these levels can derail collective efforts to reach agreed-upon goals.

Figure 2.1   Sample Plan: Selected Evaluation Questions at Five Levels

In this example, the goal for teachers' professional development is students' improved reading comprehension.

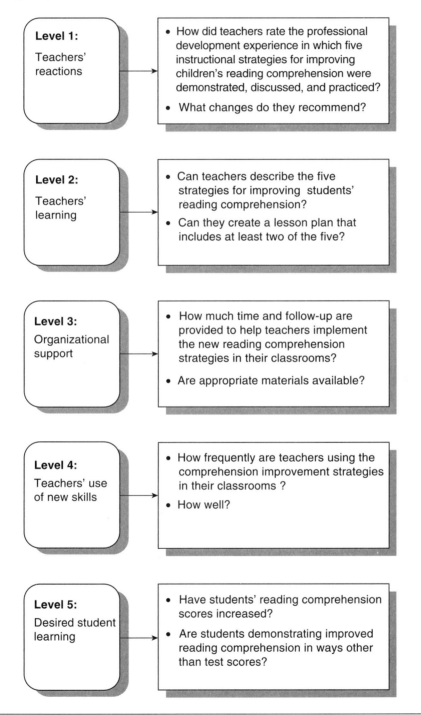

Level 1:

Teachers' reactions

- How did teachers rate the professional development experience in which five instructional strategies for improving children's reading comprehension were demonstrated, discussed, and practiced?
- What changes do they recommend?

Level 2:

Teachers' learning

- Can teachers describe the five strategies for improving students' reading comprehension?
- Can they create a lesson plan that includes at least two of the five?

Level 3:

Organizational support

- How much time and follow-up are provided to help teachers implement the new reading comprehension strategies in their classrooms?
- Are appropriate materials available?

Level 4:

Teachers' use of new skills

- How frequently are teachers using the comprehension improvement strategies in their classrooms ?
- How well?

Level 5:

Desired student learning

- Have students' reading comprehension scores increased?
- Are students demonstrating improved reading comprehension in ways other than test scores?

Because of this interdependence, it is important to assess the nature and quality of multiple tiers of contributing factors (Guskey, 2000; Killion, 2002). Evaluating the various elements related to adult learning can point to refinements and revisions warranted in the substance or forms of teachers' ongoing professional development. (See Figure 2.2.) Evaluation results can also help identify other strengths and weaknesses affecting progress toward school improvement goals (e.g., adequacy of resources, leadership, etc.).

Figure 2.2   How Evaluation Can Shape Content

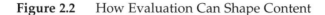

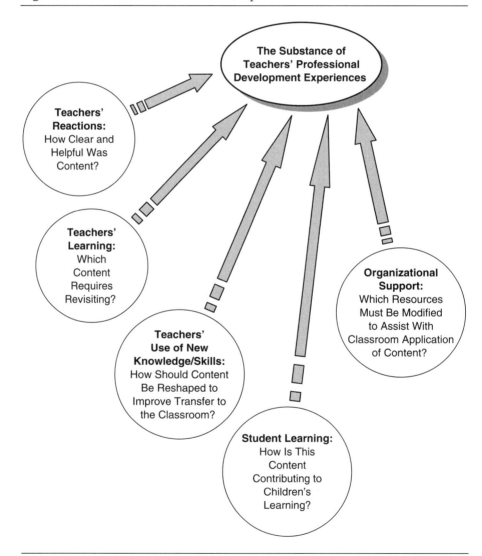

Another reason why it is important to evaluate professional development is the public interest. Gauging whether and how on-the-job adult learning makes a difference to students is especially relevant today because of the following:

1. Such initiatives represent investments of time, personnel, and money.

2. Schools depend on public funds.

3. Contemporary educators work within a political context of heightened accountability for student learning outcomes.

Accordingly, school leaders' rationale for the substance—and documentation of the success—of professional development investments are closely intertwined.

An Image of Success

Your faculty has decided to dedicate its professional development time to learning, practicing, and refining their use of five research-based strategies for enhancing reading comprehension in diverse subject areas. With your guidance, they have outlined a three-year plan that specifies the questions they will ask of themselves, of school leaders, and of their students' performance to track the school's progress toward its goals for improved comprehension. The plan also identifies the information to be collected that they agree will provide trustworthy answers to their questions at particular time intervals.

For example, to assess their own learning in the first year, teachers will use monthly grade-level meetings to share original written lesson plans that apply at least three of the five strategies to social studies. (Different subject areas are targeted in different months.) Peers will complete a short feedback form anonymously, with copies to both the teacher and grade-level team leader. The form provides a simplified rating of how true the lesson is to the research-based ideal they learned about. Its scale indicates "outstanding application," "on target," or "still needs work,"

(Continued)

(Continued)

> with additional space for suggestions and additional feedback. All grade-level team leaders will combine their ratings and feedback quarterly, to determine where and how additional demonstrations, practice, or support need to be focused for subsequent professional development.
>
> Although this example centers on evaluation at Level 2 (see Figure 2.1), the complete plan addresses all five levels. The faculty seems heartened to have found a doable means of assessing professional development that can make a real difference to their own and their students' learning. You look forward to having tangible evidence of movement toward collective goals that can help justify additional investments in the school's long-term professional development plans.

Summary of Strategies for Success

Whereas the previous chapter described two different approaches for deciding upon worthwhile adult learning content, this chapter illustrated five steps leaders can take to assess how that content is perceived, internalized, applied, and supported in actual classrooms.

As a school leader, you can help keep professional development student-centered and results-driven by doing the following:

- Connecting evaluation and content plans
- Planning backward from agreed-upon student learning priorities
- Simplifying evaluation plans to a series of thoughtful questions
- Eliciting consensus on indicators your school community will trust to provide meaningful answers to those questions

The systematic questioning strategies suggested in this chapter can also help you refine and improve the articulation of adult content foci. For example, is it really an achievable collective goal if we cannot agree on which evidence we believe would indicate success or progress toward it? Might we restate our goals in slightly different ways to facilitate assessing movement toward them?

The planned use of tiers of inquiry and relevant evidence can also inspire productive dialogue about other important educational issues. For example, under what circumstances would we want our school to establish particular substantive goals for professional development, even though they might not be measurable? How can we explain our rationale for such content to our most important stakeholders? These kinds of deliberations may help your school clarify and solidify its collective vision.

Next Steps

Together, Chapters 1 and 2 have focused on thoughtful planning, shared decision making, and the leadership you can exercise to help define meaningful adult learning content. To move forward, you and your teams must now determine the particular formats your school's professional development will take, to address that content well. The two chapters that follow shift from the what of professional development to the how.

PART II

Designing Professional Development Processes

3

Which Models Best Suit Your Goals?

Your superintendent returns from a national conference where she was so inspired by a pair of presenters that she is recommending hiring them for a full day of districtwide training. The regional educational service center is promoting teaching portfolios for professional development and will be happy to provide a free demonstration at your next faculty meeting. A nearby university informs you it has created a mentoring program that is ideal for teachers in their first three years of service. Your local teachers' association is advocating that grade-level study teams' work be counted for professional development credits toward salary advancement. And you have heard from principals in surrounding districts that mentoring, study groups, teaching portfolios, and training by recognized experts are all forms of adult learning that have been used successfully in their schools.

Although there are several issues embedded in the above scenario, this chapter centers on the questions it raises about the *design* of teachers' professional development. National standards refer to design as "process" (National Staff Development Council, 2001).

Other educators use synonymously terms such as format, models, approach, delivery, programs, or activities.

One of the more helpful distinctions to be aware of is that between process and content. It is similar to how instruction and curriculum are often differentiated when referring to student learning. That is, the former revolves around how to teach, the latter around what to learn (English, 2000). Consistent with suggestions from Chapters 1 and 2, it is assumed that you and your teachers have already determined the most appropriate *content* or substance for adult learning at your school—the what. Now the concern is *process*—the how.

What does the range of processes look like? What are their respective pros and cons? Which purposes does each serve best? Your school certainly does not have unlimited resources to expend or unlimited time to study every option.

Here are the key things to know about school-based professional development design:

1. There are essentially five models to decide among.

2. Differing rationale and premises undergird each model.

3. Three distinct ideas about alignment can help you decide which to use.

Five Models as Options

Although scores of particular designs have appeared over time, all correspond fundamentally to one of five models: (1) Individually Guided, (2) Collaborative Problem Solving, (3) Observation and Assessment of Teaching, (4) Training, or (5) Action Research (Sparks & Hirsch, 1997; Sparks & Loucks-Horsley, 1990) (see Figure 3.1).

Individually Guided

The essence of this professional development model is that teachers define and direct their own learning, much like when secondary or college students exercise options for independent study. In the purist form of this model, the teacher first determines a goal or learning objective, then decides upon a means of working toward the goal—both completely independently.

As its name suggests, individual choice and self-direction are integral to this option. What does that imply for you? For some

Figure 3.1   Five Models of Professional Development

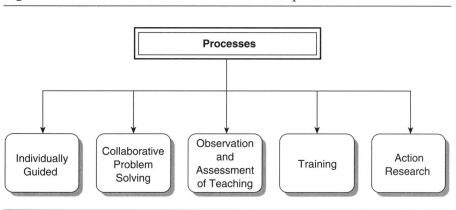

leaders, it may entail a good dose of letting go. For all leaders, it implies a lot of trust. This model is built on the premise that teachers can be trusted to—and will learn the most when they—shape their own professional development. Similar to constructivist and democratic curricular approaches for children, the idea is to build upon learners' interests to enable pursuits of questions and topics most meaningful to them (Brooks & Brooks, 1999).

What does this look like for teachers? The following are some examples (York-Barr, Sommers, Ghere, & Montie, 2001):

- Reading self-selected materials on a teaching strategy they would like to learn more about
- Journaling about dilemmas that arise on the job and warrant more thorough reflection
- Writing up ideas or success stories for publication in journals or newsletters
- Videotaping and analyzing one's own classroom instruction
- Constructing a teaching portfolio that demonstrates growth in a particular area
- Developing an individualized professional development plan for multiple years
- Attending a professional conference
- Taking or teaching a college or online course
- Leading a Teacher Center or professional association initiative

What are the major challenges associated with implementing this model? One is that teachers' individual interests and self-selected pursuits may take them in directions far different from the school's top priorities for student learning. Another is that participants may choose safe goals with scant potential to significantly advance their learning or practice. In relation, any attempts by principals to reshape individual goals can be interpreted as manipulating, reneging on, or undermining what was intended to be an independent learning opportunity.

A sound leadership strategy is to identify any requisite parameters of the independent work in writing in advance of offering this option. For example, some districts have policies or procedures specifying that individually guided goals and activities must be approved by a supervisor or linked directly to school improvement priorities. Others only support stretch goals, requiring teachers to reflect on and articulate how the independent work will enhance the teacher's existing knowledge and skills.

Another strategy to address the implementation challenges of the Individually Guided model is to clarify and delimit the school-provided time (rather than the substance) of teachers' self-selected initiatives. For example, if a district typically dedicates the equivalent of six workdays a year to professional development, it may require that at least half of them be focused on work in teams. Similarly, if a school has regularly occurring common planning time, it may identify which portion is to be used for individually guided work and which for grade-level or department collective efforts.

Collaborative Problem Solving

In contrast to individually guided professional development, the Collaborative Problem Solving model involves two or more teachers thinking and working together. It is grounded on the premise that through collaborative work, worthwhile learning will occur (Roberts & Pruitt, 2003). Constructivist theories suggesting that learning is a social as well as cognitive process provide additional grounding for the kinds of interpersonal and group discussion, dialog, and reflection that characterize the Collaborative Problem Solving model.

This design also can take a variety of forms including the following:

- School improvement or shared decision-making teams, whose charges can be broad and wide-ranging
- Curriculum development committees, with goals often more narrowly defined by content area
- Study groups, wherein teachers learn together about a topic of mutual interest (Murphy & Lick, 2001)

- Assessment teams that create tests or other measures of student learning outcomes to be used by multiple teachers (Langer et al., 2003)
- Mentoring, with a more experienced educator helping and guiding a novice teacher (Portner, 2003)
- Critical friends, wherein either pairs or groups challenge and support each other in any number of areas (Bambino, 2002)
- Student work analysis, with teachers examining samples of student work to enable improvement of subsequent instruction (Richardson, 2001a)
- Lesson study, where groups of teachers jointly create, demonstrate, discuss, debrief, and improve a particular lesson (Richardson, 2004)

A key function for school leaders is to frame as many of these collaborative work forms as possible as problem solving, that is, as efforts to resolve an issue, answer a question, or attack a problem linked to gaps in student learning. Learning theory tells us that adults are motivated to acquire new knowledge by meaningful problems to solve more so than by assigned tasks to complete (Knowles, Holton, & Swanson, 1998). Also, rallying work groups around specific, studentrelated charges can help move schools away from overreliance on standing committees whose original purposes may have been lost over time. In short, framing adult collaborations around common concerns for students can elevate relevance to, commitment from, and learning by teachers (Roberts & Pruitt, 2003).

A major implementation challenge associated with Collaborative Problem Solving (and the three other models that follow) is finding the time for two or more teachers to meet together. Addressing this challenge is so important to successful professional development that an entire chapter is devoted to leadership strategies for finding time and stretching funding to support teacher time (Chapter 7).

Observation and Assessment of Teaching

A third model of professional development also relies on teacher collaboration, but in this instance it relies primarily in pairs and is focused specifically on observations in each other's classrooms. The purpose is to serve as a second set of eyes and ears for one another for subsequent joint discussion and reflection on the instructor's teaching and students' learning.

Often this model is referred to as peer coaching or collegial super-vision (Sullivan & Glanz, 2000). However, in this context, supervision should not be confused with evaluation, hierarchy, or authority. The essence of the model is formative, rather than summative, assess-ment. That is, classroom data and feedback are provided exclusively for the observed teacher's consideration for personal growth and self-improvement. Additionally, the observing teacher can learn from being immersed in a colleague's classroom and seeing firsthand others' approaches to students, the curriculum, and instruction.

Ideally, the following three steps are included in this model (Glickman, 2002):

1. *Preobservation conversation* about what would be most helpful for the observer to focus on.

2. *Classroom observation* with some systematic way of recording information about the agreed-upon focus.

3. *Postobservation dialogue* in which the observer and the observed analyze and discuss the recorded data. Either of the two follow-ing approaches are recommended for these dialogues:
   - Nondirective, in which the observed teacher interprets the data and notes patterns, strengths, or weaknesses. The observer's role is to share the data collected and ask open-ended questions that allow the teacher to think deeply about what happened in the classroom. Nondirective approaches to postobservation conferencing are sometimes referred to as cognitive coaching (Costa & Garmston, 1994). The plan for any changes in instruction or follow-up action is exclusively the observed teacher's to make.
   - Collaborative, in which observer and observed analyze classroom data together. Either teacher may raise or answer questions, explore possible interpretations of what occurred, draw conclusions, and suggest alternatives for the next time the lesson is taught. In the spirit of continuously improving instruction and student learning, they plan together what-ever next steps are to be taken by the observed teacher (Glickman, Gordon, & Ross-Gordon, 2001).

School leaders can facilitate this model in several ways. First, provide interested teachers access to skills training for both focused data col-lection and postobservation conferencing techniques. Second, assist with the logistical arrangements necessary for reciprocal visitations.

Third, keep teacher evaluation (i.e., summative assessment by a superordinate) completely separate from the nonthreatening, non-evaluative, growth-inspiring opportunity this model is intended to be.

What are the downsides? In addition to the challenge of finding observation and meeting time, conflict can emerge over who determines the pairings that are at the heart of this professional development design. Should the choice be up to teachers themselves, the principal, or some combination of the two?

As recommended for the Individually Guided model, a sound strategy is to have written parameters specified prior to offering this option. Involving your faculty and any appropriate union leadership in developing those parameters will likely be key to successful implementation. You and your teachers will need to agree on a way to balance the principal's big picture understanding of school programs with individual teacher preferences for working with particular colleagues.

For example, your procedures might require that interested teachers propose the names of two peers, with a brief rationale for each (e.g., I value Ms. Ortega's skills in using writing workshops with seventh graders, and I am working on incorporating more of that strategy in my own subject area). The procedures could authorize the principal to judge which of the two provides both the most potential for success *and* best capitalizes on the school's overall staffing (e.g., another teacher may be more in need of Ms. Ortega's modeling and feedback).

A variation of this approach might be built around alternating years. For example, in year one of implementation, the teacher determines her own pairing; in the second year, the principal decides. In every case, of course, principals should also provide a rationale for their selections (e.g., I think it would be a worthwhile stretch for you to work with Mr. Smith, as he has had considerable experience integrating students with learning disabilities into his primary reading groups, and I know you are concerned about Margo's success in your class).

Training

In practice, this model often looks a lot like large-group, direct instruction or expert lecturing. Traditionally, it has been a format frequently relied upon for inservice teacher development. You know the scenarios. The one-shot workshops sometimes derogatorily referred to as sit-and-get. Or having a school's entire faculty assemble in an auditorium to hear a renowned national speaker make a presentation on a timely issue. Such single events and assemblies are appropriate if the goal is to inspire, entertain, raise awareness, or be exposed to basic information about a topic.

However, the Training model of professional development, when implemented fully and well, helps teachers learn new skills or strategies and, more important, apply them in their classrooms. For that reason, it is critical that savvy leaders acquire a better understanding of this model than that which they may have observed in practice historically.

There are five components necessary for training to be effective for skill acquisition and use (Joyce & Showers, 2002):

1. *Theory.* Presentation of the theory or rationale that defines the value, importance, and use of the skill. Often, this is what looks and sounds like a lecture or the equivalent of direct instruction for students. It is the telling or describing portion of training.

2. *Demonstration* or modeling of the skill, typically by the trainer.

3. *Practice.* Opportunities for learners to practice the skill, both while under the direction of experts, and over time in more natural settings.

4. *Feedback.* Timely and constructive feedback on learners' practice, so that they can understand what they are doing well and what needs further refinement.

5. *Follow-up or coaching.* Long-term guidance and assistance so that what was practiced in training sessions or other simulations is transferred to the actual work setting.

To reiterate, this five-part model is most appropriate for teaching teachers to use, or refine their use of, particular strategies or techniques. For example, how to intervene effectively when bullying or harassment occurs in the hallways; how to make history lessons relevant to contemporary middle schoolers; or how to help students comprehend more of what they read. Or, as discussed within the Observation and Assessment model of professional development, how to ask peer teachers thought-provoking questions about observed instruction.

In practice, skill training for teachers is often incomplete. It may include one or two of the elements required to be effective, but not all five. Multiple opportunities for practice with feedback, as well as follow-up over time, are frequently neglected or absent. Consequently, the anticipated change in teachers' instructional repertoire does not occur.

Prior research indicates it takes at least 20 to 25 practice trials over approximately 8 to 10 weeks to transfer moderately complex new teaching skills and strategies appropriately and consistently into classroom instruction (Joyce & Showers, 1995, 2002). Moreover, it often takes 3 to 5 years to implement changed instructional practices schoolwide (Fullan, 2001).

Statistical studies of the magnitude of gains (effect sizes) from the Training model show how different combinations of the five components impact training outcomes. The higher the effect size, the greater the gain in knowledge, skill, or transfer to actual classroom use.

For example, the data in the Knowledge column of Table 3.1 indicate that effect size increases with the addition of each training component. That is, the presentation of theory alone results in a .15 gain in teachers' knowledge of the training topic but a 1.31 gain when demonstration, practice, and feedback are added to the explanation of theory. Interestingly, when transfer to use in the classroom is the desired outcome of training (the Transfer of Training column of Table 3.1), the following is found:

> The gradual addition of training elements does not appear to impact transfer noticeably. . . . However a large and dramatic increase in transfer of training—effect size of 1.68—occurs when in-class coaching is added to an initial training experience comprised of theory explanation, demonstrations, and practice with feedback. (Joyce & Showers, 1995, p. 112)

Table 3.1 Effect Sizes for Training Outcomes by Training Components

	Training Outcomes		
Training Components & Combinations	*Knowledge*	*Skill*	*Transfer of Training*
Theory	.15	.50	.00
Theory Demonstration	.66	.86	.00
Theory Demonstration Practice	1.15	.72	.00
Theory Demonstration Practice Feedback	1.31	1.18	.39
Theory Demonstration Practice Feedback Coaching	2.71	1.25	1.68

SOURCE: Adapted from Joyce & Showers (1995), with permission of author.

What light does this information shed on the challenges of implementing this model? First, principals and other school building leaders need to be aware of the limitedness of incomplete implementation of the training process. Without follow-up and support over time, targeted skills and strategies simply will not be transferred into routine and successful use in classrooms. Effective training is an expensive, long-term investment.

Second, you should steer clear of facile overgeneralizations about teacher resistance to new strategies when this model is only partially implemented. Fullan's (1991, 2001) studies of change in schools suggest that piecemeal, fragmented, or inadequate support for improvement initiatives is much more likely the culprit in failed change efforts than is teachers' resistance. (More on this issue in Chapter 6.)

Third and most important, you need to question whether skills training should even be initiated, if it is known in advance that resources will not permit execution and support of *all five* necessary components of the model. (Revisit Table 3.1.) Relatedly, you should only employ trainers who are knowledgeable and committed to facilitating teachers' learning through processes that include presentation of theory, demonstration, practice, feedback, and follow-up or coaching over time.

Action Research

A fifth design option is variably referred to as inquiry, teacher research, action research, practitioner research, or reflective action (Dana & Yendol-Silva, 2003; Sullivan & Glanz, 2000). The simplest way to differentiate this model from the others is to think of it as teachers conducting mini-experiments, then changing some practice as a result of what is learned from the experiment. The changed practice is what makes this action-oriented research. Its teacher-directed aspects distinguish it from more formal educational research wherein teachers are more likely to be the *subjects* of empirical studies than the *initiators.*

Action research may be a solo, small-group, or whole-school professional development activity. As such, it shares characteristics of the Individually Guided and Collaborative Problem Solving models described earlier. However, those models do not require the active experimentation element.

For example, a study group (one of several collaborative problem solving formats) may dedicate itself to reading and synthesizing background literature on culturally responsive teaching strategies. It may also make site visits to schools with strong multicultural programs and develop a set of recommendations to bring to a whole faculty. This collaborative work represents worthwhile adult learning activities that can serve important school improvement goals. It is not Action Research, however . . . at least not as defined here.

In contrast, a Language Arts action researcher might teach her first period literature class using some classic book connected to traditional Western thought, and her second period class using a book with clearly Afro-centric themes. She then compares and contrasts her students' level of engagement in discussions about the books. If the data she collects suggest that one book elicits greater student interest and participation than the other, she changes her literature selections for future instruction. This is an example of action research, because it includes hands-on experimentation, data analysis, and resultant changes in practice.

In short, although it can take a variety of forms, three steps are common to the Action Research model (Dana & Yendol-Silva, 2003). One or more teachers do the following:

1. Identify a question or area of interest.

2. Collect relevant data through active experimentation.

3. Make changes based on their interpretation of the data.

What rationale can school leaders rely on to justify this design option? The Action Research model is based, in part, on the premise that we are more likely to change our practices when we are supported in exploring our own curiosities *and* when we observe and interpret what works firsthand. Additional professional development value comes in the form of more analytic and reflective teachers, within contexts that value experimentation and continuous improvement (Zeichner, 1999).

What are the major leadership challenges when implementing this model? As with the individually guided option, teachers' research interests can be quite different from the school's top priorities for student learning. Hence, I recommend the same strategies suggested earlier to structure some checks and balances between self-selected and schoolwide goals. (See end of section titled Individually Guided.)

Strategies for Deciding Among Models

Given this range of professional development options, the question then becomes, How to decide among them? As in most matters of human learning and instructional decision making, there is no magic formula that determines when to use which model. However, there are at least three ways of thinking through these choices: (1) learner alignment, (2) outcome alignment, and (3) double alignment.

Learner Alignment

One strategy is to try to match the professional development process with the adult learner. This strategy is grounded in the premise that different teachers have different strengths and preferences as to how they learn best. Some may be avid readers, able autonomous learners, or passionate writers—qualities that may make Individually Guided professional development models most appropriate. Other teachers may welcome visitors of all sorts in their classrooms, love sharing what they are doing, and exhibit keen curiosity about what is going on in the classrooms surrounding theirs . . . making the Observation and Assessment model a good choice.

In today's schools, differentiating instruction is commonly expected of teachers as a way of being inclusive and responsive to diverse students' needs and abilities (Sprenger, 2003). In simplest terms, differentiating means using multiple processes to facilitate learning, so as to increase the odds of reaching all students, regardless of their preferred learning modes. Ideally, differentiating professional development options for adult learners is desirable as well (Glatthorn, 1997).

I concur with experts who suggest that strong instructional leaders know their staffs well and through observation and communication can acquire a solid sense of teachers' learning preferences and needs (Glickman et al., 2001). Therefore, I recommend that school decisions among staff development models be informed, in part, by that knowledge. Realistically, however, a school's resources will also play a large part in determining the number and range of options available for teachers' professional development.

Outcome Alignment

A second way of thinking about professional development options is to focus on the desired learning goal (rather than individual learner attributes) and match that goal with the process most likely to achieve it (Nevills, 2003). For example, if the outcome sought is a schoolwide culture of experimentation, inquiry, and risk taking, then the Action Research model would be a sound choice. If the goal is elementary teachers' awareness of a new curriculum at the secondary level, then individually guided reading or training centered on describing and illustrating selected features may be appropriate. If the desired outcome is incorporation and adept use of a new teaching skill in the classroom, then training inclusive of theory, modeling, practice, feedback, and coaching over time is the best choice.

One reason why so many variations of the Collaborative professional development model have proliferated in recent years (e.g., examining student work together, study groups, critical friends, etc.) is that community building has become a highly valued goal. Current aspirations for schools to be more like learning communities than hierarchical bureaucracies require shared leadership, teamwork, and collective responsibility for student learning—all of which can be promoted through collaborative professional development (Lambert, 1998; Lindstrom & Speck, 2004; Roberts & Pruitt, 2003). Thus, an outcome orientation to deciding among models centers primarily on whole-school learning goals.

Double Alignment

With respect to children's learning, some authorities caution against excessively tight alignment of instruction with curriculum goals or standards. Instead, they recommend aligning teaching strategies with both standards *and* students (Strong, Silver, & Perini, 2001). Applying the concept of double alignment to adult learning means that, ideally, leaders would take both teachers' preferred learning styles *and* the desired school learning outcomes into account when making choices about which professional development models to implement.

Table 3.2 (see pp. 50–51) recaps the five models in a way that can help you decide when to choose which. The matrix highlights the models' pros and cons, as well as the purpose(s) for which each option is best used.

Table 3.2 also outlines the major challenges associated with implementing each model. I have addressed some of these in discussions earlier in the chapter. However, many challenges revolve around the resources of time and money. Accordingly, an entire forthcoming chapter is devoted to effective strategies for finding additional time and making the most of limited funds for professional development (Chapter 7).

Typical of matrix reviews, this tool is, of course, oversimplified. Ultimately, you will need to rely on your own in-depth knowledge of your staff and school, to determine the models best suited for your collective priorities, school history, and current circumstances.

Table 3.2   Tool for Deciding Among Professional Development Models

Model	Key Characteristics	Pros	Cons	Use This Option To	Implementation Challenges
Individually Guided	Teacher determines goals and activities for own learning.	Promotes individual responsibility for continuous growth. Conveys trust in teachers' abilities to make wise choices. Can motivate self-starters. Minimal costs.	Independent interests can stray from school priorities. What one wants to pursue may differ from what is truly needed; (individual blind spots).	Foster individual creativity or unique contributions to the school.	Balancing autonomous and collective goals, self-interest and the common good. Principals' attempts to reshape individual goals can be perceived as manipulation.
Collaborative Problem Solving	Two or more teachers address common concerns together.	Capitalizes on learning from each other. Promotes teamwork and collective responsibility for school priorities. Can motivate social learners.	Often requires additional training in how to work well together. Skilled group facilitators may be needed.	Discuss, propose alternatives, make decisions, or develop interventions around issues of mutual interest. Provide follow-up for the Training model.	Finding time to meet. Costs of facilitators, noncontract time, or training to optimize group relations.
Observation and Assessment of Teaching	Teachers visit each other's classrooms, record notes, and reflect together on what occurred.	Focuses directly on teaching and learning. Fosters collaboration to improve instruction. Broadens understanding of classrooms beyond one's own.	Typically requires training in collecting observation data and communicating feedback effectively.	Help new teachers. Afford veterans an opportunity for formative assessment. Provide follow-up for the Training model.	Arranging time for reciprocal visits, conferencing, and training. Costs of substitutes and training to glean the most from observations. Controversy can emerge over who gets to determine the pairings.

Table 3.2 (Continued)

Model	Key Characteristics	Pros	Cons	Use This Option To	Implementation Challenges
Training	Experts facilitate teachers' learning via: (1) Theory (2) Demonstration (3) Practice (4) Feedback (5) Follow-up assistance over time	Taps into special or state-of-the-art expertise. Can improve practice by bringing in new, alternative, or updated strategies and skills.	Trainers often limit their presentations to theory/demonstration. Requires multiple opportunities for guided practice, feedback, and support long-term to be effective.	Acquire, refine, and apply new skills or strategies in the classroom and school.	Providing on-the-job follow-up to guide and assist skill learners for 1–3 years. Finding the time and funding to sustain supports long enough for strategies to be applied capably and routinely.
Action Research	One or more teachers identify a researchable question, gather and reflect on relevant data, and initiate changes in practice based on the inquiry's results.	Encourages the exploration of practices teachers are curious about and willing to experiment with. Promotes risk taking. Minimal costs.	Research interests can stray from school priorities. May require training in how to focus an inquiry effectively.	Foster practical mini-experiments from which teachers can observe and interpret what works firsthand. Provide follow-up for the Training model.	Some release time or materials may be needed. Costs of any training to introduce the model.

An Image of Success

You and your faculty have decided upon the Training model to begin learning five strategies to help students comprehend more of what they read in varied subject areas. The first year will be devoted to the skills' introduction, demonstrations by expert users, and individual practice with critique in the protected environment of training sessions. In the second year, teachers will have a choice between two forms of follow-up support for implementing the new strategies in their classrooms: Lesson Study Groups or Peer-Expert Coaching.

Each quarter, the Lesson Study Groups will jointly create, demonstrate, debrief, discuss, and improve a subject area lesson using at least one of the research-based strategies. The school's Reading Specialist's (RS) duties will be assumed by a new Title I hire, so that she (RS) can take on the role of Peer Coach. She is one of the school's most highly respected veterans and is excited about the prospect of sharing her hands-on expertise with colleagues. Her new job description has been created together with the faculty. It includes visiting teachers' classrooms to model lessons, observing and providing feedback to those who request it, and helping teachers refine their use of the selected reading comprehension skills.

Teachers have also agreed to assess the strengths and weaknesses of the Lesson Study and Peer Coaching processes after year two, before determining how to continue or redesign supports for the third year. Overall, the staff is hopeful about the potential long-term effects of combining the three formats of training, lesson study, and coaching. Many comment that it is the most sustained support that has ever been dedicated to a particular student learning priority in their school. It is also the first time they have been given a choice about the kind of follow-up opportunities they prefer.

Summary of Strategies for Success

Although there is no simple answer to the question of which processes will work best for your school, that does not diminish the importance of the following:

- Knowing and sharing what the range of design options are
- Being able to articulate a solid rationale for each
- Understanding multiple ways of thinking about choices among models

To assist in developing each of these leadership capacities, this chapter has provided (1) succinct summaries of five different models of professional development, (2) strategies for addressing the implementation challenges of each, (3) a matrix tool to guide decision making, (4) examples of how and where teachers' and students' learning are similar, and (5) key references to pursue for additional details about any of the designs synthesized briefly here.

Next Steps

You have a sound process in place for tracking movement toward learning goals. Your teams have reached consensus on three forms of professional development. Now you must make certain that best practices are incorporated as those formats are implemented over time. In the next chapter, I provide examples and suggestions for how the effectiveness of teachers' on-the-job learning can be improved.

4

What Do We Know About Effective Practices?

You walk into the faculty workroom and a lively conversation among a half dozen teachers abruptly stops. You learn later they were commiserating about the upcoming districtwide staff development day. Several were joking about feeling scratchy throats coming on, perhaps needing to take some personal time that day. Others were lamenting how many papers they still had to grade. They predicted their time would be better spent working on their feedback for students than whatever the superintendent had planned. Some tried to retrace the last district development day, but all they could recall was how bored they felt and how little they remembered of it.

What does it take to begin to turn around critiques like these? What do we know about adult learning that can help make schools' professional development initiatives more meaningful to teachers? What characterizes effective staff development practices? These are the questions this chapter will address. And here is what you most need to understand about the answers to these questions:

1. The principles for effectiveness cut across all five models.

2. There are clear parallels between adult and student learning.

3. These parallels and principles can guide school leaders' planning, organization, and communication.

Guidance From Adult Learning Theory

Theories of adult learning provide several useful insights about motivational, instructional, and leadership strategies that can be effective with experienced professionals. This chapter focuses on five principles (Knowles et al., 1998) most relevant to supporting professional development in schools:

- Active engagement
- Relevance to current challenges
- Integration of experience
- Learning style variation
- Choice and self-direction

Active Engagement

Retention of information is greater when the learner plays an active, rather than passive, role. Reading and listening, for example, are relatively passive learner roles. In contrast, teaching others, creating useful products, and conducting demonstrations represent much more active learning approaches. Contributing to discussions or participating in site visits lie somewhere in between those two ends of the passive-active continuum.

Regardless of the professional development model(s) selected (see Chapter 3), opportunities for active engagement can increase resultant learning. What does this look like in practice? For Individually Guided models, for example, accompanying independent study with inventing concept maps to summarize new information increases one's active engagement with the material to be learned. Collaborative Problem Solving or Action Research models that include debate about alternatives and concrete plans for next steps help move participative discussions to an increased level of active engagement. Observation and Assessment models that frequently rotate observer-observed roles ensure a stronger balance between interpretative analysis and physical activity. Training models that couple initial explanations and demonstrations with learner opportunities for hands-on practice, debriefing of what occurred, and more practice, help create strong foundations for future trials in the classroom with follow-up coaching.

Overall, applying this key principle to professional development in schools means relying less on exclusively verbal presentations *to* teachers and more on active strategies of engagement *with* teachers. The latter can include brainstorming, discussion, demonstration teaching, role-playing, simulations, case study reflection or problem solving, and creative development of any number of authentic products (lessons, action plans, curricula, assessments, interpretations of data, root cause analyses, and written or oral syntheses for parents, board members, or other audiences).

Relevance to Current Challenges

Active engagement alone, however, will not ensure adult learning. Children may be captivated by high levels of activity and hands-on construction, in and of themselves. But adult learners are more discerning about the issue of engagement in *what?* To motivate or interest teachers, the substance of learning must be related to concerns, challenges, or problems encountered in their actual work lives.

What does that mean for school leaders? Your job is both: (a) to stay attuned to the current realities of teaching, and (b) to connect organizational goals and big picture priorities to teachers' concerns and interests. As Chapter 1 argued, intermittent paper-and-pencil surveys of teachers' needs are not the answer. Instead, the following examples of everyday acts can keep leaders well grounded in the realities of students' and teachers' successes and struggles:

- Earnest questioning during routine conversations
- Active listening skills
- Frequent visitations to classrooms
- Engagement with students or assisting with lessons during those visitations
- Thoughtful reflection on the *patterns* of concerns that teachers bring to you or voice at meetings
- Respectful relationships between staff and administration overall

Job-embedded transactions such as these can foster the kinds of open communication needed to increase administrators' awareness of and appreciation for the ever-changing realities of teaching.

The leadership challenge then becomes finding the common ground shared by teachers' most salient concerns and the school's most pressing needs as a whole. Addressing this challenge well takes intellectual and analytic skill. It means identifying—and being able to clearly articulate—relationships between X and Y. It requires digging beneath diverse interests to find genuine, not contrived, points of intersection. These intersections are key to making professional development content relevant to the adult learner's present realities.

In addition to current workplace connectedness, past experience is another springboard to meaningful staff development. I turn to it next.

Integration of Experience

Constructivist approaches to both children's and adult learning involve building upon prior knowledge and life experiences. Of course, one of the differences between adults and children is that the older we get the more experience we have to draw upon. That is why adult learning experts underscore the importance of valuing and integrating that more extensive experience base in the instructional strategies employed with professionals.

As before, this principle of adult learning can be applied to any of the models synthesized in Chapter 3. For example, in Collaborative Problem Solving models, teachers might be encouraged to do the following:

a. Think back to times when they were confronted with a similar challenge in either their personal or professional lives
b. Share how that issue was resolved
c. Determine how knowledge from that success or failure can shed light on today's dilemma

In Individually Guided models, prior experience and knowledge can help focus one's current growth goals by purposefully diverging from one-size-fits-all staff development content or learning activities more appropriate for others with less or different past experience.

For Action Research or Observation and Assessment models, teachers' previous experimentation or trial-and-error learning can provide the stimuli for observing self or others in the classroom, collecting data, and modifying instructional strategies. Questions applicable to either data analysis or peer coaching discussion include the following:

- What can we learn by comparing and contrasting prior and current results?
- How do past practices need to be altered to better address gaps in today's students' knowledge and skills?

Similarly, demonstrations and opportunities for guided practice within the Training model can focus on how the new skills relate to, build upon, and can be assimilated with teachers' previous knowledge and skills.

Moreover, in terms of overall organization and planning, school administrators can validate and capitalize on teachers' wealth of experience by sharing decision making about, and leadership of, staff development content, design, implementation, and evaluation.

Learning Style Variation

Like children, adults vary in their strengths and preferences regarding how they learn best. However, unlike school-aged students, teachers are likely to be more aware of their own learning style—and of mismatches between it and the professional development opportunities afforded them.

In your own career, you may have had your learning style assessed using one of several instruments popular today. For example, if assessment results suggested you were either a concrete sequential, abstract sequential, abstract random, or concrete random, the inventory used was likely Gregorc's Style Delineator (Gregorc, 1982). In contrast, The Myers-Briggs Type Indicator classifies adults along four continua: extraversion-introversion, sensing-intuition, thinking-feeling, and judging-perceiving (Briggs & Myers, 1987). A slightly different styles inventory helps determine whether you are a predominantly mastery, interpersonal, understanding, or self-expressive learner (Silver, Strong, & Perini, 2000). In sum, many tools are available to identify and shed light on personality types and learner styles.

The previous chapter introduced the idea of different learning styles and learner alignment as possible criteria for helping to decide among five general models of professional development. Adult learning theory suggests the following two additional implications of learning style variation for supporting teachers' professional development:

1. Learn more about your staff's styles.

2. Where possible, vary professional development activities according to style differences.

First, make use of the assessment tools mentioned earlier or others available from regional educational service centers and local universities. Adults typically enjoy learning about themselves and their colleagues. More important, these assessments can lead to useful insights about: (a) why adults approach educational issues from such different perspectives and (b) how workgroups and teams might be organized to take better advantage of those distinctive perspectives.

For example, if a curriculum improvement team purposefully included teachers who were mastery, interpersonal, understanding, and self-expressive learners, it might be easily sensitized to the need to design curricular opportunities that appeal to students with each of those different learning styles. In contrast, a homogeneous team might unconsciously favor solutions most compatible with the way its members approach the world and learn best.

A second suggestion for school leaders is to work to ensure that adult learning activities are varied enough to accommodate different styles. A common pitfall in professional development programming confuses topical variety/choice with learning style variety/choice. For example, a staff development initiative using a typical cafeteria prototype might offer teachers quite a wide-ranging menu of content from which to select (e.g., cooperative learning, cultural sensitivity, technology integration, school-business partnerships, senior citizen volunteers in the classroom, etc.). That is topical variety.

In contrast, if a day were organized around learning style variation, the topic might be the same for all teachers consistent with the school's highest priority content goals. (See Chapter 1.) However, varied instructional strategies would be used to address the content. For example, self-expressive or intuitive-feeling adults learn best from creative and artistic activities such as drama, open-ended discussion, and thinking metaphorically (Silver et al., 2000). In contrast, mastery or sensing-thinking learners appreciate direct instruction with opportunities to organize, repeat, and memorize information. Interpersonal or sensing-feeling learners learn best from group experiences and projects with lots of personal sharing.

In sum, strategies and activities effective for some adult learners will be less effective for others. Differentiating instructional approaches in professional development programming broadens opportunities for learning.

Choice and Self-Direction

What else does adult learning theory suggest that can help guide your school's professional development efforts? Given that adults are more self-reliant than children and more accustomed to taking charge of their own lives, it is important to allow them to shape what and how they learn. This increased self-directedness means that administrators need to partner with teachers to identify content priorities, plan and execute processes, and share leadership for ongoing staff development. It also means that opportunities for teacher choice among options should be a part of schools' professional development whenever feasible.

As with learning styles, of course, individual teachers will vary with respect to the degree of structure or direction from others they prefer or expect. (Some of the style inventories discussed earlier can provide insights about autonomy orientation.) Moreover, if your school's long-term history of professional development has been other-directed rather than teacher-directed, it is unrealistic to assume a 180-degree turnaround will seamlessly occur.

Nonetheless, as with the outcomes desired for children—that is, to become self-directed, lifelong learners—the goal is to scaffold opportunities such that teachers increasingly take charge of, and responsibility for, their own continuous education. This vision for teachers' professional development is congruent with contemporary perspectives on leadership that emphasize administrator roles as facilitators, supporters, and opportunity creators, rather than controllers or directors (Lambert, 1998; Lindstrom & Speck, 2004).

Guidance From Research on Effective Professional Development Practices

Adult learning theory suggests implications for staff development derived from knowledge about individuals and their psychology—a helpful micro-level lens. But savvy leaders need to employ multiple lenses to complete understanding of the school as a complex organization and learning community. For a complementary, macro-level perspective, I turn next to selected research that has been conducted on professional development practices in actual school settings:

- What are the characteristics of effective practice suggested by that research?
- How are they the same or different from the principles identified in adult learning theory?
- What are the limitations of the research base that school leaders should be aware of?

These questions drive the remainder of this chapter.

Findings From Studies of Teacher Learning

The most comprehensive research base pertains to Training, the model prevalent in schools historically and studied extensively by pioneers in the field of staff development and student achievement: Bruce Joyce, Beverly Showers, and their associates (Joyce & Showers, 1995, 2002). Their studies show that effectiveness increases as five key practices are incorporated cumulatively into training processes: presentation of theory, demonstration, practice, feedback, and follow-up coaching in classrooms. (See Chapter 3 and Table 3.1.)

Additional research suggests that the form or model of professional development is not what matters most (Birman, Desimone, Porter, & Garet, 2000; Garet et al., 1999). That is, traditional training in the form of workshops or institutes, as well as multiple variations of any of the other four models summarized in Chapter 3 all can be effective. Effectiveness derives not from the model but from the following five features that cut across design:

- Focus on content knowledge
- Collective participation
- Use of active learning strategies
- Coherence
- Duration

What, more specifically, does each of these features entail?

Content Knowledge

Focusing on content means targeting a staff development activity on a specific subject area or on a subject-specific teaching method, such as increasing teachers' understanding of motion in physics or of the way elementary students solve story problems in mathematics. (Birman et al., 2000, p. 30)

This finding is contrary to commonplace practices that focus adult learning initiatives on generic teaching strategies, such as using cooperative groups or graphic organizers in the classroom. It is consistent, however, with the increased expectations for student learning reflected in the contemporary curriculum standards of most states and school districts. For example, those standards often expect higher-level thinking of students and abilities to apply, rather than simply recall, information. Accordingly, teachers require deeper understanding of particular curriculum content and how students best learn that content.

When the latter becomes the focus of professional development, teachers' knowledge and skills increase.

Collective Participation

Relatedly, professional development has been found to be more effective when teachers participate in it with grade-level, subject-area, or department colleagues from their own school. Such participation contrasts with staff development structures in which teachers from different schools participate individually. Instead, collective partici- pation can beget sharing and problem solving around common con- cerns, goals, students, curriculum, methods, assessments and, often, even supplies and materials.

Active Learning Strategies

In addition to a strong subject-matter focus and collective partici- pation, effective professional development is also characterized by opportunities for teachers' active learning. This finding reinforces the idea of active engagement from adult learning theory. It is also consistent with research on training that demonstrates that hands-on practice is essential for the transfer of new skills to classroom use. Examples of active learning strategies in effective staff development include: discussion, application exercises, simulations, planning, reviewing student work, role-playing, observing or being observed teaching, and creating presentations, demonstrations, or other writ- ten products.

Coherence

A fourth feature of effective professional development is coherency. In this context, synonyms for coherence are "connection," "complement," and "fit." But what should professional development complement, fit, or be connected to? At least the following two things:

- Curriculum standards and assessments, because in education today, both directly influence teachers' work and goals
- The substance of previous professional development initia- tives, so that learning is experienced as a cumulative and recur- sive enhancement of prior knowledge

Just as strong teachers aim to link their current instruction to what came before and what is expected to follow on children's learning path, strong leaders ensure that the foci of adults' professional development opportunities are logically consistent with one another. In this respect, adult learning coherence is essentially the same as the vertical alignment schools work so hard to achieve in curricula for children. Both require keen awareness of, and attention to, connecting today's learning to yesterday's and to what is anticipated for tomorrow's. Both also require enough content overlap and reiteration to be *reinforcing*, but not so much as to become monotonous or redundant.

Duration

Last, longer duration contributes to effectiveness, because it increases the frequency of opportunities to incorporate the preceding four features: focus on depth of content, collective participation, active learning strategies, and coherence. The value of longer duration applies to both the professional development activity itself and the time span during which follow-up is supported. This finding parallels what the research on time-on-task for students indicates: More is better than less, assuming, of course, that what the learners are spending their time on is high quality.

Strategies for Success

What are some additional implications of the research and theory summarized in this chapter for the work of school leaders?

Ask Wise Screening Questions

Although you will not be the one leading every study group or facilitating many training sessions, you *will* play a large part in determining who does. Sometimes that will mean selecting from among your school's grade-level, department, or other teacher leaders. Sometimes it may involve deciding which support person to request from your district office or regional service center. Sometimes it will mean contracting with an outside consultant or university resource. And other times it may mean hiring instructional specialists, staff developers, coaches, or mentors to supplement your school's classroom teaching staff.

Each of these selection, targeting, contracting, and hiring decisions affords opportunities to ask screening questions reflective of the research and theory on best practices for adult learning.

For example, "If we were to invite you to work with us over the next 10 weeks:

- "How will you relate your focus to the other professional development initiatives our school is engaged in? (coherence)
- "Can you give some examples of how your approach addresses what today's adolescents are like? (relevance to current challenges)
- "To which subject area(s) will most of your illustrations relate? (content knowledge focus)
- "What will our teachers be hearing, seeing, and doing themselves, under your guidance? (differentiating instruction)
- "What, if any, proportion of the planned activities will have the teachers seated passively? (active engagement)
- "What, if any, products can we expect to result from teachers' work with you? (constructivist learning)
- "With which learning style(s) do you feel your approach will likely work best? (style variation)
- "Could you illustrate how you might encourage participants to connect this focus to something they are already familiar with? (integration of experience)
- "How, if at all, do you expect to group teachers? (collective participation)
- "What, if any, opportunities will teachers have to select among several different learning activities? (choice and self-direction)
- "What kinds of follow-up over time are part of what you can offer our school? (duration)"

Regardless of the models you and your teachers select, the facilitators of those models will impact resultant learning. As the questions above illustrate, both adult learning theory and the research on effective professional development practices should shape your inquiry and decision making about those facilitators.

Honor History

A common pitfall in professional development programming is faddishness, that is, frequent but temporary attachments to styles, approaches, topics, or solutions popular at a particular moment in time. Many factors contribute to this phenomenon in schools. One is educators' rightful sense of urgency about pursuing the latest interventions with potential to improve teaching and learning. Another is the American tradition of leadership career advancement through personal resumes highlighting the cutting edge contributions and strategies brought to previous organizations. And another is the commercialization of professional development, including using increasingly sophisticated marketing tools for products and services school decision makers may be too busy to vet carefully.

How can school leaders avoid the bandwagon pitfall? Honoring the history of your school's professional development initiatives is a solid place to start. That requires learning about the 5-to-10-year background of both content and processes relied upon. It means affirming, connecting to, and building upon those processes and content, rather than ignoring, discounting, or summarily replacing them—or proceeding as if you were starting with a blank slate.

First, learning theory suggests that integrating adults' prior experience and knowledge can increase both motivation to learn and new learning. Valuing history and linking present-day initiatives to your school's previous professional development are means of honoring teachers' *collective* experience while avoiding overestimating today's trends.

Second, several studies have found that coherence is an important part of effective professional development practice (Birman et al., 2000; Garet et al., 1999). Coherence-building involves reinforcing what came before by making transparent the similarities and differences with new knowledge or current directions. Articulating these connections well is such a critical communication skill that I will revisit and expand upon it in the next chapter.

Qualify Assertions

Grand claims and overgeneralizations about potential impact are additional factors contributing to faddishness and *in*coherence in teachers' professional development in schools. What are some antidotes to these commonplace practices?

One is more careful scrutiny of prospective providers' offerings. The questions delineated earlier in this section are useful screens for making informed judgments about potential.

Another is a more highly nuanced understanding of what is known about adult learning and effective practice. As reflected in this chapter, the current knowledge base relies more heavily on theory, professional consensus, and expert thinking than on conclusive results from empirical study (Guskey, 2003a). For example, I cannot say with certainty that there is one best design for teachers' professional development, or that Collaborative Problem Solving models have been proven to lead to greater learning than Action Research models. Although Training has been studied rigorously over time, other professional development formats have not. Moreover, much of the recent research on effective practice has focused on mathematics and science teaching with no assurances that those findings apply equally well to other subject areas or contexts (Guskey, 2003c).

It should not be unexpected that there remain many unknowns about things as context-dependent and complex as leadership, human learning, and adult development. What are some practical implications of these unknowns for your work?

- Acknowledge limitations
- Temper assertions appropriately
- Rely on solid sources

Again, transparency is key. Acknowledging that current understandings are limited and constantly evolving should be a part of leaders' communication about choices and directions. When conclusive or quantifiable empirical results are not available, it is eminently reasonable to ground rationale on the best thinking of expert educators and theorists. In those cases, however, leaders' language should make such distinctions clear. Notice, for example, the escalating certainty denoted in the following expressions:

a. This successful initiative in my school shows that . . .
b. Current professional consensus suggests that . . .
c. Surveys of experts in this field conclude that . . .
d. Research has repeatedly found that . . .

Discerning readers should become familiar with these writing conventions and what they connote for the strength of claims. School leaders should monitor and adjust their own language, to accurately represent the varying degrees of (un)certainty conveyed in the professional literature.

Additionally, you can make the most efficient use of your limited reading and information-gathering time by targeting resources of reputable research and practitioner organizations. An example of the former is the American Educational Research Association (AERA); and of the latter, the National Staff Development Council (NSDC). Relying on information published or endorsed by either of these two national associations is a smart way to stay current with the ever-evolving knowledge bases relevant to supporting teachers' professional development.

National Standards for Professional Development

State and school district curriculum standards define what experts and other influential stakeholders consider most important for children to know and be able to do. Similarly, national standards also exist for adult professional development in schools (see Table 4.1, p. 68). As mentioned in the Preface, this book is designed around questions that reflect and illustrate the following three things that school leaders most need to know about current national standards for staff development:

- Content
- Processes
- Context

As with most quality standards, it can be expected that these will be revisited and revised in the future, both to capture advances in knowledge and to inspire the field to ever-higher levels of performance.

What does this mean for the work of school leaders? It underscores the need to stay current with the research and best thinking on effective staff development practices. One way of doing that is through your professional affiliations and networks. A brief synopsis of salient information you should know about the National Staff Development Council (2004) follows.

The NSDC is a nonprofit professional association whose mission is to enhance student success through high quality staff development and school improvement. It is a large, national organization with over 10,000 members, an annual conference, and numerous publications, projects, workshops, and academies. It serves as an international network and resource provider. Its services include customized facilitation and consulting for individual schools and districts. Its *Journal of*

Table 4.1   National Standards for Staff Development

CONTEXT STANDARDS

Staff development that improves the learning of all students:

- Organizes adults into learning communities whose goals are aligned with those of the school and district. (**Learning Communities**)
- Requires skillful school and district leaders who guide continuous instructional improvement. (**Leadership**)
- Requires resources to support adult learning and collaboration. (**Resources**)

PROCESS

Staff development that improves the learning of all students:

- Uses disaggregated student data to determine adult learning priorities, monitor progress, and help sustain continuous improvement. (**Data-Driven**)
- Uses multiple sources of information to guide improvement and demonstrate its impact. (**Evaluation**)
- Prepares educators to apply research to decision making. (**Research-Based**)
- Uses learning strategies appropriate to the intended goal. (**Design**)
- Applies knowledge about human learning and change. (**Learning**)
- Provides educators with the knowledge and skills to collaborate. (**Collaboration**)

CONTENT

Staff development that improves the learning of all students:

- Prepares educators to understand and appreciate all students, create safe, orderly and supportive learning environments, and hold high expectations for their academic achievement. (**Equity**)
- Deepens educators' content knowledge, provides them with research-based instructional strategies to assist students in meeting rigorous academic standards, and prepares them to use various types of classroom assessments appropriately. (**Quality Teaching**)
- Provides educators with knowledge and skills to involve families and other stakeholders appropriately. (**Family Involvement**)

SOURCE: National Staff Development Council (2001).

Staff Development is published quarterly, and focuses on articles "written primarily by practitioners who bring a real world attitude to the challenges of school improvement and organizational change" (NSDC, 2004, p. 4).

An Image of Success

The follow-up support to initial training has already begun. Both Lesson Study and Coaching participants are linking their work to the curriculum standards tested statewide in four subject areas. The Coaching specialist gently pushes teachers who have been successful implementing a comprehension improvement strategy in one subject to move forward to work on an additional subject the ensuing week. The Lesson Study groups built subject matter rotation into their work right from the start. Sixty percent of responses to your open-ended survey on the comprehension improvement initiative indicate teachers feel they are learning as much about the social studies, language arts, science, and math standards for their grades as they are the new reading strategies. This is good news.

Lesson Study groups are integrating more brainstorming and role-playing into their meetings to vary the problem-solving techniques with which they began their collaborative work. You have also noticed some cross-fertilization between the two support formats. For example, sometimes the Coaching specialist writes up a lesson she wishes to use as a model for a particular grade level. A Lesson Study group dedicates one of its sessions to examining the lesson as if it were a case study. They then forward their suggestions to the Coach in writing. The groups are finding that committing their feedback to writing helps them more clearly focus and refine their ideas about applying the reading comprehension strategies. And the interaction between the two support formats is making the Coach feel less like a lone ranger on the move constantly from one classroom to another.

Overall, teachers continue to be appreciative of and motivated by the hands-on, follow-up support to initial training. They feel their professional development efforts are producing real work they can use with their students almost immediately.

Summary

This chapter began with a vignette reflecting teachers' perceptions of a district's professional development programming as a forgettable and unproductive use of their time. The chapter then proceeded to offer examples and suggestions for how the effectiveness of teachers' on-the-job learning can be improved by increasing the following:

- Active engagement learning strategies
- Relevance to current challenges
- Integration of prior experience
- Attention to learning style differences
- Focus on subject-matter knowledge and pedagogy
- Collective participation
- Coherence
- Duration of learning activities and their follow-up

These suggestions and examples were derived from adult learning theory and selected studies of professional development practices that expand teachers' knowledge and skills.

Next Steps

Research-based content and processes are being integrated into your school's staff development initiatives. To move forward, you must also help build and sustain a schoolwide environment conducive to adult learning. I devote the remainder of this book to practical steps principals can take to create supportive contexts for teachers' professional development.

PART III

Creating Supportive Contexts

5

How Can Leaders Focus Improvement Efforts?

When you arrived at this school two years ago, teachers were participating in study groups to research differentiated instruction appropriate to their grade levels. Many staff continued to volunteer for the Teacher Expectations and Student Achievement (TESA) training that the regional service center provides each fall. About a third of the faculty were opting to develop teaching portfolios around either brain-based learning or interdisciplinary curricula, in lieu of the annual classroom observation by an administrative evaluator. Senior staff was mentoring eight new teachers on classroom management. And, when you examined closely the school's recent history, you saw that professional development opportunities had included: creating PowerPoint presentations, violence prevention, inclusive education, critical thinking, interpreting standardized test scores, dealing with elder care, appreciating diversity, identifying child abuse, using graphic organizers in the class-room, understanding the state retirement system, integrating technology, as well as other educational issues. No wonder some teachers were feeling pulled in myriad directions.

Fragmentation, disorientation, and dilution of focus can easily creep into the adult work environment when ambitious improvement efforts accumulate over years. Professional growth experts agree that neither powerful, student-centered *content* (Chapters 1 and 2) nor brilliantly designed *processes* (Chapters 3 and 4) alone will ensure successful teacher development in schools. Favorable *contexts* are also needed (DuFour, 2001, 2002b; NSDC, 2001; Peterson, 2002). And such contexts require leaders to tend carefully to nurturing the overall school environment in which successive improvement initiatives accrue (Zmuda, Kuklis, & Kline, 2004). Terms often used interchangeably with context are the school's "climate," "culture," "atmosphere," "environment," or "systemic conditions."

Making sense of numerous initiatives, building coherence among them, and sustaining focus on priorities are just a few of the ways that principals contribute to creating supportive contexts for continuous adult learning (Burnette, 2002; Guskey, 1997). This chapter is the first of three dedicated to explaining and illustrating strategies for cultivating and maintaining such environments. All three chapters are grounded in the following premises:

1. Leadership shapes context.

2. School contexts either help or hinder development efforts.

3. Principals are uniquely positioned to see how countless pieces contribute to—or detract from—the whole.

Strategies for Success

Every school has numerous and varied programs, goals, special projects, partnerships, and hopes (Fullan, 2001; Hall & Hord, 2001). With them, often come related professional development opportunities for teachers. Chapter 1 elaborated a gap analysis model useful both for identifying top priorities for student learning and for connecting adult learning content to those priorities. Chapter 2 provided examples of five different types of questions that can guide ongoing assessment of how your school's planned improvements may be affecting teachers, their classroom instruction, and their students' learning.

Yet even the most enlightened planning, monitoring, and readjustment practices need to be supported with continuing leadership focus, direction setting, and coherence building. Why? Because what professional development expert Thomas Guskey stated almost 10 years ago remains equally true today:

> The primary task that lies ahead is not so much to generate new ideas as to integrate them; not so much to find individual ideas that work as to make a collection of ideas work together. (Guskey, 1997, p. 144)

How can you help your school make sense of and integrate a collection of improvement efforts? What steps can leaders take to replace fragmentation and overload with coherence? How can principals facilitate understanding of and commitment to the school's big picture priorities? This chapter addresses these and other questions relevant to how leaders sustain focus on agreed-upon improvement goals, while nurturing supportive contexts for professional growth.

Integrating Improvement Initiatives

To set the stage for the strategies you can employ to build coherence, I begin with some analogies to teaching and learning.

From their work in classrooms, most teachers know from experience that it takes a combination of elements to help students progress. They know, for example, that it may take one approach to motivate some children, quite a different approach for others. They know they need: a planned direction for daily lessons, longer units, entire years, instructional materials, and different ways to teach and reteach important concepts. They know the atmosphere created in their classrooms affects their students' attitudes and learning. They know that learning activities or materials that are relevant and engaging to one group of students may be experienced as exactly the opposite by another and, therefore, require reworking. They know that some children are quick to draw their own connections between one set of ideas and another. They are also aware that other students benefit immensely from the teacher making those relationships explicit and reinforcing the connections regularly.

In sum, most teachers understand that child development is complex and multidimensional. They understand student learning requires bringing to bear varied resources and efforts simultaneously.

Capitalize on Parallels to Classrooms

As a building leader, you may be able to counteract staff perceptions of professional development as fragmented by drawing parallels between the understandings summarized earlier and the complexities of whole-school improvement. That is, like classroom teaching, school improvement aimed at increased student learning also requires bringing multiple elements to bear simultaneously (Killion, 2002). Those elements often involve: the curriculum, assessments of learning, teaching techniques, motivational strategies, school climate, materials, discipline, leadership support, and more.

In other words, what may initially appear to be disconnected or fragmented foci, may in fact reflect efforts to address concurrently the many interrelated contributors to student learning. Accordingly, some professional development initiatives may center on instructional techniques (e.g., five strategies for improving reading comprehension). Others may focus on motivating and engaging students (e.g., understanding how brains are wired differently or how preferred learning styles vary). Some initiatives may center on the curriculum (e.g., articulating a K–12 sequence of math skills development). Still others may address students' readiness to learn (e.g., identifying and intervening for suspected child abuse or inadequate nutrition). And some may focus on teachers' readiness to teach (e.g., helping novices manage their classrooms; orienting faculty to the new science textbook series).

Although multitasking within one's own classroom is taken for granted, some teachers will need help connecting the dots among the grade level, department, and schoolwide professional development initiatives in which they are expected to participate. What can leaders do to make those connections more apparent? One strategy is to draw attention to the parallels between the classroom and the school with regard to simultaneous and complementary interventions on multiple fronts. For example, use your own words to convey and reinforce a message such as the following:

Principal: "It's clear you give attention every day to what to teach, how to teach, sustaining students' interest, developing and reworking materials, and creating a safe and welcoming atmosphere in your classroom. Similarly, as a school, we are also attending to those wide-ranging responsibilities, each of which contributes a piece to student learning. That range shows up in the collective activities that drive our study groups, curriculum teams, action research projects, coaching programs, and other staff development initiatives. Instead of viewing those activities as pulls in different directions, I encourage you to think of them as you do your varied daily classroom efforts. That is, as complementary parts that work together to help students learn."

Of course, ongoing reinforcement of connections through verbal messages is just one tool for building coherence. Visual images that demonstrate relationships can also help. I turn to this strategy next.

Create a Framework

Principals and other school leaders may hold a sharp image in their minds of how multiple improvement initiatives are working together. Transposing that mental image into a graphic organizer can help others visualize and make sense of the school's big picture as well.

Diagrams, concept maps, charts, and figures of various sorts are powerful tools for framing, synthesizing, and illustrating the relationships among what individual teachers may experience as piecemeal programs and disconnected expectations (Guskey, 1997; Marzano, Pickering, & Brandt, 1990). Visual aids can clarify connections, reduce complexity to more manageable terms and, perhaps most important, demonstrate coherence around shared improvement targets (Killion, 2002).

Like maps and photographs, graphic organizers are often also amenable to expansion, compression, insets, and overlays that afford diverse narrow- and wide-angle views. Figure 5.1 (see p. 78), for example, illustrates some of the elements discussed earlier that contribute to classroom learning. Figure 5.2 (see p. 79) builds upon the Figure 5.1 perspective by adding examples of selected professional and organizational development foci that relate to each of those classroom contributors.

Together, the two concept maps are intended to clarify the linkages between whole-school improvement activities and student learning goals. They also are meant to demonstrate the parallels (mentioned earlier) between taken-for-granted multitasking within classrooms and the multiple development initiatives being implemented across the building.

Some may disagree with the concepts selected or positioning of relationships within these sample figures. The major point is that an explicit framework can contribute to shared sense making of whichever principles and priorities best capture your school's current context. Admittedly, the analysis and synthesis of schoolwide efforts can be a rigorous intellectual challenge. Fortunately, today's computer technology makes tailoring appropriate circles, boxes, arrows, labels, or other graphic representations relatively easy.

It is important to underscore that the creation of such frameworks is a *leadership* responsibility. As principal, you will typically have

Figure 5.1   Selected Contributors to Student Learning

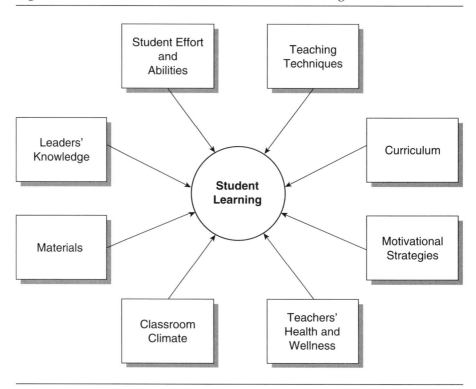

access to more complete information than is available to others about the countless activities taking place within the school. Moreover, the providers or facilitators of individual professional development processes may not consistently articulate how their specific focus relates to other initiatives being undertaken in the school. Instead, expert consultants and proponents of particular professional development programming often intentionally highlight the uniqueness and superiority of their own preferred content or design (Guskey, 1997). Hence, framing, articulating, and illustrating the congruence among the elements in the big picture is left to the principal.

Introduce Initiatives in Terms of the Framework

Although not all facilitators can be relied upon to situate their particular emphasis within the school's overarching improvement framework, you can. In fact, as a building leader, you should be your school's most ardent and consistent reinforcer of how the many parts contribute to the whole. You should also be the building's key articulator of how current school directions relate to, differ from, or build upon previous initiatives (Zmuda et al., 2004).

Figure 5.2   Sample Framework Linking Adult and Student Learning

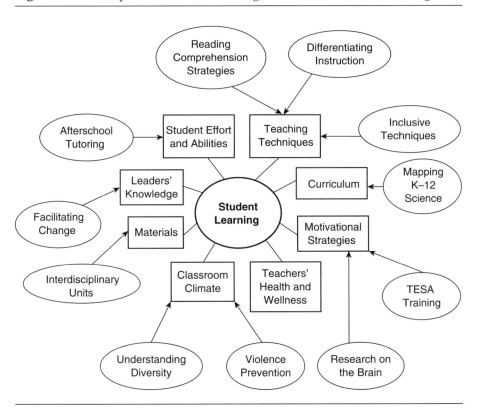

One strategy for accomplishing these kinds of integration is for you to personally *introduce* as much of the ongoing professional development work in your school as possible. This means playing a highly visible role, showing up regularly at lots of different group meetings, and actually delivering the words of introduction for that day's activity.

It is assumed that your school's professional development work will be ongoing and take a variety of forms (see Chapter 3). So what your introduction will look and sound like will also vary. For example, it may involve stopping by at the start of your fifth-grade teachers' bimonthly meetings to develop common unit tests to say a few words about how integral coordinated assessment is to the school's priorities for students' reading comprehension. It may mean displaying your graphic framework on a projection screen for a larger work group to point out how and where a particular training session fits within the constellation of the school's improvement efforts. It may involve emphasizing the previous experience of a particular facilitator team in addressing your school's highest priority student learning goals before turning over the leadership of a study group to those facilitators.

In exercising these important communication roles, moving beyond glib generalities is crucial. The elements that comprise your school's framework—and the specific rationale behind them—should drive your message. That is, explanations of why you are here should draw upon your school's unique challenges, resultant student learning priorities, and selected improvement initiatives (see Chapter 1). Your framework should help you avoid resorting to popular (but oftentimes cliché) aphorisms such as "so that all students will learn" or "to leave no child behind." Instead, a much more focused and meaningful rationale is, for example, "because we've agreed that improving students' reading comprehension across the curriculum is our number one goal this year."

In sum, brief but purposeful introductions at ongoing professional development work sessions can accomplish the following:

- Highlight connections to broader school foci
- Reduce fragmentation and increase coherence among different groups' work
- Demonstrate the principal's commitment to shared goals
- Reinforce the school's direction

Regularly referring to the framework can elevate the general sense of its value and utility as an integrating tool for the school. Moreover, principals' *modeling* of introductory comments that relate individual professional development initiatives to collective improvement goals can pave the way for similar expectations of other school leaders and facilitators. The following is an example:

Principal to department chair, peer coach, or other staff developer: "I'd like to help kick off the first three meetings of your action research teams by articulating how the teams' work links to and supports the school's current learning priorities. For sessions beyond that, I'll expect you to take over that role. Please let me know how I might be able to help you to become as comfortable as possible providing that bigger picture context."

The goal is for more and more teacher leaders and staff developers to share responsibilities with you for reinforcing schoolwide foci and demonstrating connections among initiatives. In moving toward that goal, a sense of increased coherence and improved integration can become embedded in your school's culture.

Apply Framework in Other Routines

Cultivating supportive school cultures for continuous adult learning, of course, requires more than intermittent reminders within professional development introductions. A companion strategy is to underscore your school's improvement framework through other everyday leadership acts as well.

For example, additional venues for reiterating priorities, sustaining focus on selected improvement initiatives, and building awareness of the coherence among those initiatives include the following:

- Regular faculty meetings
- Student assemblies
- Presentations to school boards
- Ad hoc conversations with members of the public
- Reports to accrediting or other governmental agencies
- Newsletters to parents
- Local press releases

With respect to external relations, capitalizing on these venues can expand the wider community's knowledge of your school's efforts to change for the better. Internally, when teachers see that the logic and rationale for their professional development are systematically incorporated into ongoing exchanges with other stakeholders, their own understandings of and commitments to improvement goals can increase.

Relatedly, public relations experts often recommend that leaders maintain at the tip-of-the-tongue three concise bullet-points that convey key messages they wish to routinely promote (Conners, 2000; Kinder, 2000). Advance reflection and readiness with such messages allows taking advantage of whatever communication opportunities may emerge during the workday. Again, a clear and integrative conceptual framework can assist with preparing cogent key messages.

Use Framework as Screening Tool

So far, my emphasis has been on using improvement frameworks as communication tools. I have presented them as vehicles for coherence-building and as graphic means of collective sense making. Both aim to diminish possible perceptions of fragmentation and incongruence among numerous demands.

But the value of creating an integrative framework for professional development goes beyond improved communication. A clear framework can also serve as a screening tool for decision making. For example, you and your shared leadership teams can use this tool to carefully examine proposed initiatives for their compatibility with existing programming. (e.g., How, if at all, is that discipline technique congruent with the motivational strategies we have been integrating into our classrooms in the recent past?) Such use represents a kind of vetting aid for screening new things *in*.

In the reverse direction, the screen can also be employed to weed *out*, modify, or discontinue extant initiatives that, when viewed in the context of the big picture, no longer fit well (e.g., Doesn't our study groups' work on comprehension improvement strategies incorporate enough information on learning styles so that we can let go of our distinct programming around students' learning styles?). These examples use the framework as a qualitative screen of the *substance* of proposed and ongoing development activities.

In order to work well together, professional development initiatives should (a) share common premises and goals, (b) complement rather than compete with each other, and (c) address the school's top-priority student learning goals (Guskey, 1997). In short, the content of your staff development initiatives must truly *be* complementary in order for either the oral or visual communication strategies suggested above to be meaningful. The graphic display of multiple elements in close juxtaposition can help reveal substantive congruities, incongruities, overlap, or redundancy.

A comprehensive improvement framework will also make readily apparent any excessive clutter. In this way, the graphic can be a useful screen for the *quantity* of ongoing initiatives. If, for example, you discover there are simply too many distinct professional development emphases to display, then it is time for renewed prioritizing. There is a point at which enlarging the size of the paper on which the framework is constructed is no longer feasible! In fact, then, your teachers *are* being pulled in too many directions. And no amount of verbal or graphic sense making can effectively counteract such overload. Instead, you and your teams should return to the kinds of gap analysis and self-study detailed in Chapter 1 to refocus the school's priorities and reestablish clear direction.

Sustaining Concentration on Goals

Thus far, this chapter has suggested and illustrated the following five strategies for integrating the multiple improvement initiatives of which teachers' professional development is a part in most schools:

- Capitalizing on parallels to classrooms
- Creating an improvement framework
- Introducing initiatives in terms of the framework
- Applying the framework in leadership routines
- Employing the framework as a decision-making tool

Using these strategies, principals can help ensure that combinations of development efforts work together and are well understood. Such understandings can displace the sense of fragmentation, incoherence, and overburden that often impedes progress toward achieving student learning goals.

Nevertheless, integration represents just one approach to focusing your school's collective improvement efforts. A second, slightly different approach requires leaders to help sustain teachers' concentration on agreed-upon goals. The latter involves both support and pressure (Fullan, 2001). Three ways of exercising these leadership responsibilities are presented next.

Develop Guiding Questions

As described in Chapter 3, many contemporary forms of staff development are based on teachers learning from one another in pairs or small groups. Yet "principals must do more than organize teacher teams and hope for the best" (DuFour, 2001, p. 15). To sustain concentration on schoolwide priorities, leaders can specify parameters for teachers' collaborative work in the form of guiding questions.

Often, the questions can be identical or similar to those developed with staff when planning for professional development evaluation around top-priority student learning targets (see Chapter 2). For example, "What are additional instructional strategies we can use to improve students' reading comprehension in social studies? What feedback can we provide each other that might help us optimize those strategies in the classroom? What are we learning about students' reading comprehension from the common assessments we have been using in science instruction?"

Sometimes, principals and other school leaders can develop questions that help link varied initiatives around improvement targets. For example, "What would a lesson incorporating third-grade science and reading comprehension standards look like? Have other schools developed a performance assessment to take the place of a paper-and-pencil quiz on that lesson? How can we integrate what we are learning about multiple intelligences and multiculturalism into the state-required unit on regional history?"

Regardless of the forms that professional development may take at your school in any given year, guiding questions can help sustain focus on agreed-upon priorities. They can also prevent teachers from wasting precious learning time wondering "Why are we here?" or "What are we supposed to accomplish?" (Burnette, 2002, p. 53).

Expect Products

A related means of focusing time and attention is to request a tangible product responsive to the guiding question(s). Examples of possible products include: summaries of action research findings, rubrics to guide the evaluation of student work, outlines of lessons or units created, samples of common assessments, reports on student achievement with strategies identified to improve future results, improvement plans for a particular grade level or content area, videos of teachers practicing new instructional techniques, written reflections on the experience of observing another's teaching, synopses of the results of collaborative problem solving, and portfolios of relevant artifacts (Burnette, 2002; DuFour, 2001).

The product should be tailored to the format and purpose of the professional development work. Additionally, identifying an authentic audience for the product can influence its shape and quality. As appropriate, you should encourage teachers to envision audiences other than either you or themselves, alone. Clear expectations for material outcomes not only help teams focus, but address school-wide needs. Productive professional development can result in useful contributions to the work of other grade levels, departments, and teams. As more and more teachers experience tangible benefits from the school's professional development efforts, support for and commitment to shared improvement goals can increase.

Structure Two-Way Communication

Another way to promote teachers' focus on agreed-upon goals is to structure communication systems between you and the various professional development work groups dispersed throughout the school (Burnette, 2002). For example, you might ask each group to select a member to serve as liaison to the building's administration. Or you might require that written feedback be forwarded to you from each group at some specified, regular intervals (e.g., every two weeks; every two months).

You and the groups should define in advance the nature of the updates that either the liaison would communicate in face-to-face meetings with you, or that would be collected in writing. (See Table 5.1.)

Table 5.1   Sample Feedback Form for Work Groups

Professional Development Group Name: _____

Date: _____

- Student learning priority your group is working on?

- Guiding question(s) your group is addressing?

- Where you are now in response to the question(s)?

- Problems the group is encountering?

- Resources or other support requested from building administrators?

- Principal's response:

Through either of these vehicles, teams could report where they were in relation to the guiding questions or student learning priorities driving their work. Groups could also identify problems they were encountering and suggest resources or other support needed from you (Burnette, 2002).

To sustain such communication systems long-term, you would need to respond to group updates and suggestions quickly and constructively. The information forwarded to you should influence your decisions about when to attend a particular group's meetings, what kind of clarification or motivation might be needed to keep the group's work on track, and how to modify the balance of leadership pressure and support for each group's efforts.

An Image of Success

Lesson Study teams are starting to accumulate so many strong examples of curriculum units that the media specialist has organized the lessons for sharing through the school library by cross-referencing the samples by subject area, grade-level suitability, and type of reading comprehension strategy illustrated. You wrote a brief preface attached to each lesson, highlighting the connections to school goals for student learning. Your message also acknowledged the teams' hard work.

At your urging, the veterans who had been mentoring new faculty on classroom management techniques shifted their emphasis. Currently, they spend much of their time guiding the novices on their use of the comprehension strategies. Several new teachers told you that, now that some of their troublesome students are understanding more of what they read, they seem to be acting out less in the classroom.

All the hours you spent creating a graphic framework to illustrate the relationships among your school's various improvement initiatives finally paid off. You and your School Improvement Committee used the framework as the centerpiece of a persuasive presentation to the superintendent and central office staff developers. The result: Your school will be allowed to concentrate its professional development time on follow-up activities supporting the reading comprehension priority in lieu of attending the upcoming districtwide staff development day programming.

Summary

This chapter centered on steps principals and other school leaders can take to focus a building's improvement initiatives, including teachers' professional development. Many of the steps revolve around helping staff "cut through the noise and clarify, 'this is what is important . . . this is what we strive toward'" (DuFour, 2002b, p. 61).

As principal, you can illuminate and regularly reinforce what your school is striving toward by doing the following:

- Developing a framework that integrates improvement efforts
- Using the framework for communications and decision making
- Providing structures that keep collective focus on agreed-upon goals

As illustrated in this chapter, (1) making sense of numerous initiatives, (2) building coherence among them, and (3) maintaining concentration on student learning priorities are just a few of the ways that school leaders contribute to creating and sustaining a child-centered, supportive culture for adult learning.

Next Steps

Positive contexts are so critical to adult and student learning that principals must approach building them from multiple angles. Now that you are successfully focusing and integrating your school's improvement efforts, you must fine-tune your systems for facilitating changes long-term. The next chapter shares several strategies for addressing teachers' inevitable concerns and ambiguities about changed practices.

6

How Are More Enabling Cultures Shaped?

As part of your own professional development, you are participating in a year-long Principals' Academy cosponsored by the state administrators' organization and a local college. One of the Academy's requirements is that participants visit at least three schools outside their district and report back on their observations. During the debriefing of reports, the group was struck by how frequently observations centered on the distinctive feels of the various schools. Typically, visitors recounted that they got the feel of a school within just a short time of entering the building, wandering about, and observing relatively few students, staff, offices, and classrooms. Most participants could clearly identify whether the atmosphere they experienced was positive or negative—an environment in which they would feel good about working or not.

Research confirms the observations portrayed in this vignette: School cultures are not neutral (Fullan, 2001). Instead, they either facilitate or impede student and adult development (DuFour, 2001). Moreover, school cultures are often experienced as perceptible personas (Peterson, 2002). Those personas both reflect and shape the way school members think, feel, and act.

Put another way, any organization's cultural context mirrors the values and unwritten expectations characteristic of "the way we do things around here" (Deal & Peterson, 1999). And leadership plays a key role in influencing the ways students and teachers do things in a particular building (Lambert, 1998; Peterson, 2002).

To supplement the strategies suggested in Chapter 5, this chapter describes and illustrates additional steps you can take to create and sustain supportive contexts for school improvement. More specifically, the chapter addresses the questions: What distinguishes hospitable climates for teachers' professional development? How can principals and other school leaders enhance the positive, and dilute the toxic, aspects of a building's culture? What tools and processes have been shown to help with such reculturing (Fullan, 2001)?

Central to savvy leaders' grasp of these issues are the following:

1. School cultures evolve slowly but continuously.

2. Improvement means change for the better.

3. Change can be uncomfortable.

Enhancing Systems of Support

What distinguishes nurturing environments for teachers' professional growth? Positive school contexts are characterized by shared understandings, coherence, and sustained focus on school improvement targets. The relationships between professional development content and priorities for student learning are clear. School leaders' communication and decision making are guided by those priorities. Adult learning takes a variety of forms, while staying true to school-wide foci through guiding questions and two-way communication between teachers and administrators. Together, these elements harness collective energies in a clear direction toward agreed-upon goals.

In contrast,

> Schools with toxic cultures lack a clear sense of purpose, have norms that reinforce inertia, blame students for lack of progress, discourage collaboration, and often have actively hostile relations among staff. These schools are not healthy for students or staff. (Peterson, 2002, p. 11)

Strategies for Facilitating Change

One approach to fostering collective responsibility for student learning *and* a healthier overall school environment comes from 30 years of research on change (Hall & Hord, 2001). That approach, the Concerns-Based Adoption Model (CBAM), provides school leaders a framework and several tools for facilitating change successfully.

In this section, I discuss two of the tools. The first is geared to diagnosing and addressing professional concerns about change, termed Stages of Concern (SoC). The second is aimed at enhancing momentum toward a well-articulated vision of the improvement(s), called Innovation Configurations maps. My explication of these tools is synthesized from the research, theory, and implementation work of CBAM developers and experts: Shirley H. Hord, Gene E. Hall, Susan Loucks-Horsley, William Rutherford, Leslie Huling-Austin, and the Southwest Educational Development Laboratory (Hall & Hord, 1987, 2001; Hord, Rutherford, Huling-Austin, & Hall, 1987; Roy & Hord, 2003). Their insights are applied here to teachers and schools, although CBAM is relevant to other organizations as well.

Tailor Support to Stages of Concern

SoC is grounded in several premises. First, most teachers experience predictable concerns about doing something new or different. Second, effective change facilitators systematically expand their awareness of those concerns. Third and most important, leaders respond to adults' concerns, thereby increasing both commitment to and successful implementation of school improvement goals. Each of these three foundations is explained below.

What is predictable? There are seven distinct stages of concerns that fall into several general categories.

Figure 6.1 reflects teachers' feelings as they engage with changed instructional practices or programs. At Stage 0 (Awareness), the teacher either does not want to learn about the change or is simply unaware of it. Stage 1 concerns reflect curiosities about what is new (Informational). Stage 2 captures teachers' concerns about how the change may affect them (Personal). The personal and informational concerns of Stages 1 and 2 both center on the Self.

In contrast, Stage 3 centers more on the work (Task) than the Self. At this point, teachers are participating in or trying out the proposed change, and logistical concerns of various sorts are emerging. Often, their questions at this stage revolve around time, resources,

Figure 6.1　　Stages of Concern

Stages of Concern		Expressions of Concern
IMPACT	6 Refocusing	I have some ideas about something that would work even better.
	5 Collaboration	I am concerned about relating what I am doing with what my colleagues are doing.
	4 Consequence	How is my use affecting students?
TASK	3 Management	I seem to be spending all my time getting materials ready.
SELF	2 Personal	How will using it affect me?
	1 Informational	I would like to know more about it.
	0 Awareness	I am not concerned about it.

SOURCE: Hall & Hord (2001, p. 61). From Gene E. Hall & Shirley M. Hord, *Implementing Change: Patterns, Principles, and Potholes.* Published by Allyn and Bacon, Boston, MA. Copyright 2001 by Pearson Education. Reprinted by permission of the publisher.

assistance, or skills needed to perform the task or implement the program.

Within the final general category (Impact), feelings shift away from Self and Task toward concerns for the change's effects on students. Three distinct stages comprise the Impact category. Stage 4 focuses on how to make the change work better for students (Consequence). At this stage, teachers may be interested in modifying or adapting the change to match what they know about the children in their charge. Those interests may lead to questions about impact beyond one's own classroom. Stage 5 concerns (Collaboration) center on how to increase the benefit to students by working on the change together with other colleagues. And lastly, Stage 6 (Refocusing) reflects teachers' feelings of having successfully worked with the change and witnessed the effects on children. At this stage, they are thinking creatively about implementing other changes to make the original one work even better for students.

Before proceeding, a caution about SoC is warranted. For ease of understanding, stages are explained above in a linear, sequential fashion. Not surprisingly, real life in schools is more convoluted. Only some teachers will move through all the stages of concern or do so in ascending numerical order. Most will skip around, experience several concerns concurrently, and move along the continuum in different directions at different times.

How do effective change facilitators elicit concerns? Although some teachers will share their frustrations and interests with you unsolicited, CBAM experts suggest additional means of expanded sampling of concerns. The first is "one-legged interviews." This term refers to simply asking teachers questions during the chance meetings that occur in hallways and other common areas throughout the normal workday. These are brief, informal conversations. They are most productive when questions are specific to the change, for example:

> How are your students managing the new math manipula-tives? If a teacher answers, "I haven't really had a chance to use those," the teacher is at the first stage, awareness, not really concerned about the innovation. [In contrast] A teacher who answers, "Mary Jo and I have been working on some ways to let the students use them more for discovery" has reached the collaborative stage. (Holloway, K., 2003, p. 2)

A second, more systematic way of eliciting concerns is through written, open-ended inquiry at the beginning, end, or during profes-sional development activities. For example, in the course of a study group's information-gathering about a secondary-level reading com-prehension instructional strategy, participants can be asked, "What, if anything, concerns you about the new strategy?" Responses are col-lected and examined for patterns of individual and group concerns.

The third and most rigorous means of gathering information about concerns is a 35-item survey questionnaire developed by CBAM researchers. This tool is most appropriate for those interested in build-ing and analyzing statistical data. It is not recommended for our pur-poses here, or for anyone who has not been trained in its technical use.

What does responsiveness to SoC look like in practice? A primary reason for seeking to understand teachers' concerns is for change leaders to be able to *tailor* ongoing and follow-up support as effec-tively as possible. Your goal should be to bring to bear whatever help will "resolve the concern and move the person toward more advanced use of the innovation" (Hall & Hord, 2001, p. 65). Resolving concerns can mean anything from validating teachers' efforts, creating classroom coaching opportunities, or providing additional materials, to changing schedules, reassigning support personnel, and recognizing or celebrating successes. The key is to align the intervention with the level of the concern.

Though there are no simple formulas for making those matches, SoC experts provide the following examples (Hall & Hord, 1987, pp. 361–364):

Stage 0, Awareness concerns*
    a. Acknowledge that little concern about the innovation is legitimate and appropriate.
    b. Share some information about the innovation in hopes of arousing some interest in it.

Stage 1, Informational concerns
    a. Provide information contrasting what the teacher is presently doing with what use of the innovation would entail.
    b. Create an opportunity to visit a nearby site, classroom, or school where the innovation is being used.

Stage 2, Personal concerns
    a. Encourage innovation use gingerly; do not push unnecessarily.
    b. Provide access to a change facilitator who can assist in use of the innovation.

Stage 3, Management concerns
    a. Offer "comfort and caring" sessions, where experienced teachers provide advice and assistance with specific management concerns.
    b. Provide answers in ways that easily address the small, specific, "how-to" issues that are the cause of the concern.

Stage 4, Consequence concerns
    a. Forward written information about topics that might be of interest.
    b. Advertise the teacher's potential for sharing skills with others.

Stage 5, Collaboration concerns
   a. Arrange a meeting between the interested individuals for idea exchange.
   b. Create opportunities for them to circulate outside their present situation and work with others who may be less knowledgeable.

Stage 6, Refocusing concerns
   a. Encourage the individuals to take action with respect to their concerns.
   b. Provide them with access to the other materials they think may help and encourage them to pilot test these to find out if, in fact, they would be of use to others.

A caveat about stages and interventions. So far, I have emphasized the usefulness of SoC for tailoring responses to the inevitable concerns that arise in change processes. However, knowledge about the predictability of concerns can be applied in more proactive ways as well. SoC should also shape decisions about designing and adjusting the sequence of *content* for teachers' professional development (see Chapter 1). For example, since task concerns more typically appear prior to impact concerns:

> Teachers with intense task concerns don't want to hear about the philosophy; they want help in making the innovation work more smoothly. The more abstract and subtle aspects of innovation use are of greater interest to teachers with impact concerns. (Hall & Hord, 2001, p. 61)

In sum, both *anticipating* and responding to concerns are important leadership responsibilities. Each contributes to creating supportive contexts for teachers' professional development and other school improvement initiatives.

Use Innovation Configurations Tools

Other CBAM tools for facilitating change are Innovation Configurations (IC) maps. IC maps are precise verbal descriptions of what the new practice or program looks like when in use in the classroom or school. These descriptions specify the critical components of the desired change. As applied here, their primary purpose is to help teachers clearly visualize the expected outcome of the professional development initiative in operation.

How do IC maps contribute to creating supportive school contexts? A lucid, well-articulated vision of the improvement can enhance collective movement toward it. Collective movement fosters momentum. And an atmosphere of *momentum* toward shared goals is stimulating and energizing. Moreover, the collaborative process of creating IC maps can generate grassroots understanding, clarity, and enthusiasm for the vision—also contributing to a more favorable environment for growth.

What do IC maps look like? Historically, IC maps have taken a variety of forms, including checklists and narrative profiles with bullets indicating ideal, acceptable, and unacceptable use. Expert contemporary illustrations of IC maps often look like the rubrics teachers use for evaluating student work. That is, they are charts with discrete columns that capture a range or continuum of variations. Within each column, active verbs are used to create word pictures of the varying degrees to which an individual performance approaches a preidentified ideal. Those individuals can be students, teachers, principals, or whoever else is desired to be part of the change process.

For example, Figure 6.2 centers on the teacher. Consistent with research on effective staff development, the desired outcome is that the teacher "participates in professional learning that impacts depth of understanding." (This principle was discussed in Chapter 4 as

Figure 6.2   Sample Innovation Configurations Map for the Teacher

DESIRED OUTCOME 8.2: Participates in professional learning that impacts depth of understanding.			
LEVEL 1	**LEVEL 2**	**LEVEL 3**	**LEVEL 4**
Exhibits deep understanding and meaning of new concepts and strategies. Solves problems and adapts new strategies to match classroom circumstances.	Exhibits deep understanding of new content knowledge and uses new strategies routinely.	Gains an understanding of new content knowledge but cannot translate that understanding into new practices.	Gains awareness of new content knowledge and skill but not deep understanding.

SOURCE: Roy and Hord (2003, p. 38). Reprinted with permission of the National Staff Development Council, www.nsdc.org, 2004. All rights reserved.

Figure 6.3   Sample Innovation Configurations Map for the Principal

DESIRED OUTCOME 4.1: Analyzes with the faculty disaggregated student data to determine school improvement/professional development goals.

LEVEL 1	LEVEL 2	LEVEL 3	LEVEL 4
Works with the whole faculty to analyze a variety of disaggregated student learning results to determine school improvement goals, plus student and adult learning needs.	Works with a representative group of faculty members to analyze disaggregated student achievement data to determine school improvement goals, plus student and adult learning needs.	Analyzes disaggregated student data alone and informs the faculty of the results and needs.	Uses personal experience and opinion to determine school improvement and staff development goals.

SOURCE: Roy and Hord (2003, p. 74). Reprinted with permission of the National Staff Development Council, www.nsdc.org, 2004. All rights reserved.

content knowledge.) The Level 1 column describes the ideal, while the other levels capture natural variations that are likely to occur but that are less and less like the desired outcome.

In contrast to Figure 6.2, Figure 6.3 is designed from the perspective of the principal. Consistent with the information presented in Chapter 1, this IC map is built around a different desired outcome. The change desired is that the principal "analyzes with the faculty disaggregated student data to determine school improvement/ professional development goals." Again, Levels 2 through 4 portray distinct pictures of how far there remains to go for the principal to reach the ideal outcome.

Though these two examples (Figures 6.2 and 6.3) depict four levels of variation, IC maps may be constructed to capture whatever number of levels seems most appropriate to a particular change initiative. The distinct levels reflect the reality that, during the extended process of learning and implementing new practices, individuals modify and adapt those practices. IC maps summarize and display the preferred direction of those adaptations with each level representing another step toward optimal use.

How are IC maps developed? CBAM experts recommend a collaborative process for drafting, pilot testing, and refining IC maps with teachers. They estimate that it often takes a full week for three to seven key people to jointly construct a first draft.

Three questions should drive the IC development process:

1. What does the innovation look like when it is in use?

2. What would I see in classrooms where it is used well (and not as well)?

3. What will teachers *and* students be doing when the innovation is in use? (Hall & Hord, 2001, p. 49).

The following are suggested steps for addressing these questions thoroughly:

- Studying all available information on the ideal version of the change, including consulting with experts
- Observing a variety of classrooms where the changed practice is in use
- Deciding what the critical components of the practice are
- Determining how the components cluster into incremental variations between the ideal and the least desirable (see the levels in sample Figures 6.2 and 6.3)
- Reaching consensus on the wording of components and variations (note: Figures 6.2 and 6.3 each describe one component and four variations)
- Pilot testing the first draft in classrooms, to see how well it reflects the various patterns of use observed
- Modifying or clarifying components and other wording as a result of piloting
- Sharing IC maps with all teachers, facilitators, and other potential users of the new practice

Overall, the major goal in writing each component description and each variation description is to be as visual as possible. The better the word pictures, the easier it will be for teachers, principals, and others to see what successful use of the innovation entails (Hall & Hord, 2001, p. 42).

The most helpful word pictures are built around *action* verbs that succinctly capture the essence of the change. One of the purposes of pilot testing IC drafts is to make sure that those actions are *observable* in the natural setting of classrooms. And one of the purposes of including teachers in the IC development process is to ensure that the map's wording is understandable and the actions doable in the eyes of the innovation's users.

How else are IC maps useful? So far, I have emphasized the value of CBAM Innovation Configurations for nurturing environments conducive to learning by clearly mapping successive steps toward desired results. As such, IC maps serve important visioning, communication, and culture-building functions. But they are useful in other ways as well.

Teachers can use IC maps as guides and reminders of agreed-upon goals for personal growth plans or teaching portfolios, in Individually Guided forms of professional development. (See Chapter 3's five models). In this way, ICs serve as supplementary tools for beginning with the end in mind and for linking individual and collective aspirations.

Teachers can also use IC maps for peer coaching and Observation and Assessment models of professional development. Peer or facilitator feedback and dialog about observed levels can help shape future performance. And collaborative problem solving around IC maps can be aimed at moving toward Level 1 configurations of desired changes.

Additionally, principals and other change leaders can use IC maps to monitor and assess schoolwide progress toward improvement goals. Aggregated data on where staff tend to cluster on IC maps can be used to reshape the kinds of resources and other aids provided to help teachers advance to the next level. For example, change facilitators might create additional opportunities for demonstrations, guided practice, and classroom coaching of instructional components that IC maps show to be less well implemented. In this way, IC status information supplements Stages of Concern data, to help school leaders *tailor* ongoing interventions and supports to keep change processes moving forward.

Rethinking Resistance to Change

The previous chapter emphasized strategies for focusing improvement efforts, building coherence among multiple initiatives, and maintaining concentration on selected student learning goals. The reason for recommending those strategies before those in this chapter was the research finding that

The greatest problem faced by school districts and schools is not resistance to innovation, but the fragmentation, overload, and incoherence resulting from the uncritical acceptance of too many different innovations. (Fullan, 1991, p. 197)

In contrast to conventional wisdom about blockers or resisters to new initiatives, Fullan's work shifts attention from change-averse individuals to the broader environment in which changes are introduced. This is a different way of thinking about why the improvements that building leaders embrace may not take hold schoolwide. Fullan's perspective suggests that resistance to change is more likely a *symptom* than a *cause* of systemic problems.

The SoC and IC tools and strategies illustrated in this chapter suggest a slightly different way of thinking about resistance as well. That is, CBAM experts view resistance to change as predictable and understandable aspects of Stage 2 (Personal) or Stage 1 (Informational) concerns. When change is introduced, it is natural and typical to feel uncertainty, ambiguity, lack of clarity about what is happening, or self-doubt about being able to succeed with the new practice. CBAM strategies such as one-legged interviews and mapping ICs place the emphasis on change facilitators' listening to, observing, legitimizing, and addressing the concerns of teachers expected to alter their practices. In this model, change leaders are expected to demonstrate empathy, monitor concerns, and take action to adjust supports to those concerns.

These CBAM approaches are built, in part, on the premise that facilitators' failure to adequately address concerns at lower levels inhibits prospects for advancement to ideal levels of implementation. For example, insufficient resources, and downplaying or ignoring teachers' informational or personal concerns, can leave the school stuck in a configuration of the change far removed from the desired outcome.

Worse yet, such neglect can *inspire* resistance to the initiative. This insight from CBAM experts (such as Fullan) shifts the perspective away from viewing resistance exclusively as a quality of unwilling individuals. Instead, resistance may also be understood as a result or symptom of what is going on in the broader change context—in this case, the adequacy of leaders' support and facilitation.

In sum, smart principals should appreciate varied perspectives on resistance to change including those that point toward the school's systemic coherence and leadership as contributors. That said, even the most renowned school improvement authorities acknowledge that "Of course, there always are real resistors" (Hall & Hord, 2001, p. 72). Hence, principals should be aware of multiple strategies for creating and sustaining supportive school cultures, while deterring individual resistance from becoming schoolwide negativity.

Strategies for Minimizing Resistance

CBAM researchers have shown that tailoring supports to Stages of Concern and helping teachers clearly envision change targets with Innovation Configurations are two ways of diminishing resistance. Others follow.

Maintain Supports for Sufficient Time

Even in the most nurturing environments, changes in classroom practice typically take three to five years to be fully implemented (Hall & Hord, 2001, 1987). Momentum plateaus, dips in performance, conflict, confusion, and reluctance to continue are inevitable parts of such extended processes (Fullan, 2001, 1991). Even if key facilitators change during that time, leadership support throughout the entire process is critical. That means that new principals will need to pick up where their predecessors left off to build upon the efforts that have already been put into initiatives aimed at student learning goals (see section of Chapter 4 titled Honor History).

Without such continuity, the commonplace resisters' argument for nonparticipation because "this too will pass" will be validated. The antidote to such arguments is the *demonstration* of ongoing leadership support for the initiative. Concrete ways of demonstrating support include the following:

- Allocating time and other resources (e.g., Is it really a priority if time and resources are *not* dedicated to it?)
- Communicating frequently and enthusiastically about the continuing importance of the initiative
- Celebrating any positive results related to the change (e.g., improved student performance, outside recognition, increased grant funding)

Address Conflict Directly

Leaders also need to bring differences out into the open so that they can be resolved (Janas, 1998). Teachers and administrators should be invited to voice and negotiate issues by addressing together questions such as: Where are we in the process? Where do we want to end up? How will getting there help us meet our top goals for student learning? What is impeding us from getting there?

Such one-on-one and small-group discussions can be guided by the gap analysis work done earlier (Chapter 1), the evaluation questions and criteria previously agreed upon (Chapter 2), and the improvement frameworks developed to reinforce coherence among initiatives (Chapter 5). After all, one of the purposes of that prior work was to clarify and refine a shared direction for school improvement. If part of the resistance stems from having veered from agreed-upon priorities, or from feeling undersupported in pursuing them, then school leaders should want to hear about how, where, when, and why.

Openly airing concerns and differences can provide principals with valuable information about emerging conflicts and frustrations before they become overwhelming barriers to progress. For example, teachers may "legitimately resist change required by a program that is poorly designed, underfunded, or focused on unnecessary activities" (Janas, 1998, p. 11). Hearing out staff is essential to eliciting this kind of feedback. Additionally, this example illustrates that opportunities to articulate the underlying reasons for resistance can serve constructive purposes.

Counteract Stories of Failure

Resistance is often perpetuated in the negative anecdotes that are shared among staff about "the last time we tried something like that" or in comments criticizing forms of teacher learning other than trial-and-error in one's own classroom (Peterson, 2002). How can you help prevent such accounts from dominating the school's culture? By "finding examples of success to counteract stories of failure . . . and replacing negative stories of professional development with concrete positive results" (Peterson, 2002, p. 15).

Again, careful listening is the first step. Your antidotes will be more effective if they address the specifics of the toxic account. For example, if the essence of the negative anecdote is that "teaming never works around here," you need to have at the tip of your tongue several current examples of which departments or grade levels are collaborating successfully. Wherever possible, include illustrations of how their teamwork helped students or contributed to other school improvement priorities.

The point is not to disparage any individual's interpretation of history, nor to pretend that missteps have not occurred. Rather, the goal is to maximize communication about productive efforts and positive outcomes, to ensure that balanced and hopeful stories predominate in the broader narrative that is your school's context.

Model Hopefulness

As a school leader, your language, actions, and attitudes are constantly on display. You can capitalize on that high visibility among teachers by consciously modeling openness to change.

For example, your reactions to state mandates or district directives will be easily observed by staff. If you frequently demonstrate opposition, or routinely lament "what's coming from downtown," you might be serving as the perfect role model for resisters in your own building. In contrast, if you search for the common ground among state, district, and building initiatives, and exhibit receptivity to all sources of potential improvement, you will be modeling the constructive attitudes expected of your school's students and staff.

Of course, critical thinking is also an important part of strong leadership. Leaders sometimes increase their credibility by refraining from exclusively Pollyannaish stances. In fact, change leaders "reflecting publicly and straightforwardly on their own doubts and resistance to change may . . . give other stakeholders a chance to identify with someone going through the difficult process of change" (Janas, 1998, p. 12).

Again, balance is key. Overall, a school's culture will be enhanced by its principal's positive worldview. Leaders' modeling of hope, energy, and opportunity-thinking rather than obstacle-thinking can be another way of diluting the influence of resisters.

An Image of Success

Classroom coaching is going very well. Teachers report that they look forward to their one-on-one problem solving with the school's former reading specialist. With the new Innovation Configurations maps now in use, coach-teacher pairs are able to focus their observations and reflections more sharply than before. As a result, their discussions and plans for refining comprehension strategies are becoming increasingly helpful to classroom teachers.

You have decreased the number of full-faculty meetings from biweekly to once a month. This change provides more opportunities for you to participate in Lesson Study groups or meet with new teachers and their mentors. When faculty meetings do occur, you start by dedicating the first 5 minutes to updating staff on concerns that have arisen about the ongoing reading improvement initiative. You then proceed to share the steps taken to ameliorate common implementation problems and to brainstorm additional ideas to address the concerns. Teachers have become accustomed to checking the school's shared bulletin board (or its electronic version) to stay current on information you would have conveyed previously through more frequent whole-school meetings.

Overall, you sense some collective momentum and growing enthusiasm for the changes put in place to support the school's academic targets. Other principals in the district have started to request information about what they hear is going on at your school. Personally, you've never felt more energized by your leadership work here.

Summary

This chapter opened with a vignette about the palpable nature of a school's climate and culture. It then proceeded to recommend a number of strategies you can use to build and sustain a nurturing environment for teachers' professional development and other improvement initiatives.

Lessons learned from research on successfully facilitating change in schools confirm that principals are key to shaping "the way we do things around here." Exercising that influence in a positive direction means

- Collaboratively mapping what successive steps toward desired results look like
- Understanding the concerns that naturally accompany new practices
- Tailoring support to those concerns
- Sustaining supports for at least three to five years

The chapter also included strategies for diminishing resistance to change. Throughout, expressions of resistance and concerns were primarily viewed as potentially useful feedback to help leaders fine-tune efforts to create more supportive cultures for learning.

Taken together, Chapters 5 and 6 have focused on the everyday acts of leadership that can shape the school environment in positive ways. The emphasis has been on communication and visioning strategies, collaborative relationship-building, and persistent attention to student learning priorities.

Next Steps

Along with the influence you exercise daily through your interactions with students and staff, you have implemented several key processes for ensuring that improvement initiatives are moving forward. Now you need to pull together more resources to sustain the school's momentum. I turn next to the crucial contextual resources of time and funding.

7

How Can Resources Be Optimized?

As you enter your third year as principal at this school, the mood of the building seems to have changed for the better. You have built solid, trusting relationships with staff and community. Team leaders have come to respect—and frequently emulate—your positive, problem-solving approach to daily challenges. Staff are generally pleased a clear direction has been established. Most students are responding well to the school's higher expectations of them. And your School Improvement Committee's plans are actually being read and referred to by teachers, rather than just sitting on shelves gathering dust. In fact, many teams and faculty have expressed willingness to do even more, but there just never seems to be enough time.

How have schools created more time for teachers' professional development? What are some steps leaders can take to generate support for changed staff or student time in school? What strategies are available for making the most out of limited professional development funding?

This chapter answers these questions by providing examples and syntheses of state-of-the-art thinking on the critical technical matters of time and money. What school leaders need to keep in mind about these issues are the following:

1. Time is a key instructional resource.

2. Teacher time is an investment with significant costs.

3. Using time effectively is more important than creating additional time.

Strategies for Making Time

Studies of schools and districts over the past 15 years reveal essentially four strategies for making time for teachers' professional development:

- Schedule common planning time
- Reduce teachers' contact time with students
- Bank teachers' contact time with students
- Buy additional time

While there is some overlap among the strategies, I discuss and illustrate each separately, for ease of understanding (see Table 7.1). The information in this section is derived primarily from the research syntheses of Richardson (2002) and Watts and Castle (1993).

Schedule Common Planning Time

This strategy is aimed at coordinating schedules so that grade-level, department, interdisciplinary, or other targeted groups of teachers can work together during the regular school day. The strategy assumes that each teacher, either by contract or tradition, is already allocated a certain amount of planning or preparation time each day or week—that is, time without student contact.

One administrative challenge is to arrange targeted teachers' planning times to coincide. At the elementary level, this is often accomplished by scheduling *pull out* resources, such as music, physical education, the arts, library, or computer lab, at times that free up the targeted teachers simultaneously. At the secondary level, common time for targeted teachers may be factored into the master schedule of course offerings.

Table 7.1   Assessing Options for Making Time

Strategy	Advantages	Disadvantages	Leadership Challenges
Schedule Common Planning Time	Time to collaborate during regular workday. Students do not lose instructional time. Uses existing personnel. No change for families.	Decreases teachers' individual planning time during workday. Typically treats specialty subject teachers differently.	Arranging targeted teachers' schedules to coincide. Negotiating how much common time to be used for professional development.
Reduce Teachers' Contact Time With Students	Time to collaborate during regular workday. Some forms require no change for families. Potential student enrichment from special experiences.	Students lose face-time with regular teacher. Political and financial costs of using substitutes. Forms affecting school start-dismissal times can inconvenience parents. Personnel and transportation costs for some special programs.	Persuading community stakeholders of value of professional development during regular workday. Ensuring that special/substitute programming is high quality.
Bank Teachers' Contact Time With Students	Time to collaborate within each workweek. Students' instructional time does not change. No new personnel costs.	Additional transportation costs likely. Irregular school start-dismissal times can inconvenience parents.	Hiring and scheduling bus drivers for different hours on different days. Coordinating transportation districtwide. Persuading community stakeholders of value of professional development built into each week.
Buy Additional Time	Financial incentives can motivate some teachers. Investment in professional development can signal commitment to teachers' learning.	Costs of new hiring or staff stipends. Political and financial costs of using substitutes.	Persuading community stakeholders of value of professional development investments.

Even when schedules are synchronized, another leadership challenge is to negotiate how much of the common planning time is to be dedicated to professional development. For example, at Ball High School in Galveston, Texas, teachers have a 90-minute conference or prep-period daily. (The school uses a block schedule.) Two of those prep-periods a month are used for professional development. At the third- through eighth-grade levels at Madison Park School in Phoenix, Arizona, teachers agreed to use two of their five prep-periods a week for grade-level teamwork.

An advantage of the common planning time strategy is that collaborative forms of professional development can become a part of teachers' regular workday. Other benefits are that students do not lose any instructional time, and no additional personnel costs are incurred. Another advantage is that, from parents' and caregivers' perspectives, there is no change in the regular school days' starting and stopping times. A disadvantage is that special-areas staff (such as physical education, music, etc.) may not have the same opportunities as other teachers. Another downside is that teachers' individual planning or preparation time—a scarce commodity in most school workdays—is decreased.

Reduce Teachers' Contact Time With Students

This strategy involves freeing up selected teachers from a portion of their usual contact time with students, so that they (the teachers) can participate in professional development during the regular workday. Sometimes this is accomplished by arranging for other adults to cover targeted teachers' classes. Replacements may include existing paid or nonpaid personnel, such as teaching assistants, other support staff, college interns, administrators, community volunteers, or members of teaching teams.

Another way to free up some teachers' time is through programming that can accommodate large groups of students. Examples include: theater performances, assemblies of various sorts, or special presentations by business volunteers, older students, or community groups.

A slightly different model for freeing up teacher time can be used in schools with substantial vocational, school-to-work, or community service expectations for students. For example, if those off-campus activities were scheduled for the same day or half-day each week, teachers' regular classroom instructional responsibilities for a significant block of time would be eliminated.

These strategies' primary advantage is that, because not all teachers would be needed to supervise such programs, some are freed up for professional development opportunities during normal school hours. Like the common planning time approach, this strategy can maintain traditional school day start and dismissal times, thus ensuring predictability for parents and caregivers. Another potential benefit is that children's school experience could be enriched by some of the programs mentioned earlier.

The downsides are that *someone* still has to organize, coordinate, and oversee any large-group or off-site programming for students. Inevitably, there are personnel and transportation costs for such alternatives. Also, typically, even when other adults cover classes, regular classroom teachers still have to plan the lessons for that time, thereby decreasing some of this strategy's appeal as a time creator. Moreover, legal and political problems often come into play when persons other than certified professionals are used to substitute in classrooms. And, importantly, the quality of classroom instruction may suffer in the regular teacher's absence.

Another approach that frees up teachers while avoiding the downsides delineated earlier is to create regularly scheduled late-start or early-dismissal days for students. For example, students' classes at Brandon High School in Ortonville, Michigan, begin at 11:00 A.M. each Wednesday, while teachers arrive at 7:30 A.M. to collaborate in professional development. In Ellisville, Missouri, the Rockwood School District has early-release days for students one day a month to create professional development time for all teachers in the same quadrants of the district. Iowa City, Iowa, releases students an hour early every Thursday, to provide an extended block of time for adult professional development on those days.

Late-start and early-release approaches assume that schools already exceed the minimal number of instructional hours/days that the different states require. Nonetheless, significant disadvantages also accompany this strategy. For one, parents', caregivers', and bus drivers' schedules are disrupted by intermittent school day alternations. And, more important, students' total instructional time is reduced.

Bank Teachers' Contact Time With Students

Banking minutes and hours is a strategy for creating blocks of time for professional development without reducing students' total instructional time with their regular teachers in any given week. This approach can take a variety of forms. The common denominator among them is that not every school day begins and ends at the same time. Often, extended instructional time during four days of the week is saved (deposited, in banking terms), so that it can be withdrawn on a fifth day, when students either arrive later or leave school earlier than the other four days. The deposited and withdrawn minutes leave the weekly balance of instructional time for students even.

For example, at Addison Elementary School in Marietta, Georgia, the school day starts 10 minutes earlier and ends 10 minutes later than it had in the past, for four days a week. Those 80 minutes of banked instructional time were exchanged for releasing students from school at 1:30 P.M. on Wednesdays, so that teachers could participate in professional development each Wednesday afternoon. Some high schools follow similar banking models, but schedule later arrival times (rather than early release) for students on the fifth day.

The major benefit of this approach is that all teachers can be afforded a significant block of time for professional development activities within the normal workweek. Importantly, students' contact time with their regular teachers is safeguarded. Financial costs are not incurred because the total number of employment hours remains the same. Also, this strategy makes adult learning time a permanent part of each week, thus signaling the value of and commitment to teachers' continuing development.

Administrative downsides include the logistics of scheduling buses and hiring drivers amenable to different hours on certain days. Additionally, altered school starting and ending times can create significant burdens for working parents and caregivers. Accordingly, moving toward such schedules requires extraordinary leadership efforts to consult, involve, and communicate effectively with numerous stakeholders, including community members.

Buy Additional Time

The most expensive of the four strategies for making time for teachers' professional development involves several forms of purchasing additional staff time. Some forms are variations of strategies previously discussed. For instance, additional costs are incurred when common planning, early starts, or late departures for teachers are created by employing substitutes or other new support staff (rather than reducing students' instructional time or covering classes with existing personnel).

In Montgomery County, Maryland, a specially designated staff development substitute teacher is hired for each school. That person does not cover the classes of teachers who are sick or needing personal time away from school, but substitutes exclusively for teachers requesting professional development time for part or all of a day. At Madison Park School in Phoenix, Arizona, two full-time substitute teachers are dedicated solely to freeing up teacher time for professional development during the regular workday. These examples are the equivalent of adding one or two teaching positions for a school. Other schools might create *substitute banks* of 30 to 40 days a year, again particularly earmarked for expanding teachers' professional development time. Those days can go even further when half-day substitutes are permitted.

A different form of buying time is to pay teachers stipends for participating in professional development during summer, other vacation, evening, or weekend time. Reimbursing teachers for individual graduate courses taken or awarding salary raises for the accumulation of advanced degrees may also be considered forms of buying time for teachers' professional development. Also, some districts award inservice credits for professional development work completed on teachers' own time. This is a form of buying time, in that the credits are typically converted (eventually) into supplementary monetary compensation.

Adding days to the annual employment contract is another way of buying time. For example, in New York State, several full days of professional development are interspersed throughout the school year, typically in October, January, and March. Students do not attend classes those days, and the time is considered a normal part of teachers' employment calendar.

Several of the advantages and disadvantages of strategies discussed previously also apply to buying time. For example, while substitute teachers allow professional development to occur during normal school hours, their frequent use can be troublesome to students and parents. Moreover, teachers typically need to create lesson plans and prepare materials for their subs, calling into question how freeing the substitute time is.

Overall, a key benefit of buying time is that stipends, reimbursements, and credits for teachers can be incentives to participate. Also, much-needed additional time for teachers' professional development can be created through such investments. The major downside is that most school districts' budgets are already dominated by personnel costs, and it is often difficult to convince taxpayers of the value of investing even more.

Leading Processes for Making Time

Prepared with ideas for making time for professional development, school leaders often also require strategies to facilitate decision making about changing staff and student schedules. The following suggestions can help (Richardson, 2002):

- Give teachers a strong voice in exploring options and planning any changes. Share with them the possibilities described earlier and the examples of actual schools that have implemented different strategies for making time. Invite them to brainstorm other possibilities that might work for your school. Involve teacher associations, unions, and collective bargaining leaders early in the process.
- Estimate together how much time is warranted, for how many teachers, and at what intervals, for the goals and models of professional development your school has chosen. You may need to address questions such as: How heavily is your school relying on Action Research or Observation and Assessment models that require time within the regular workday? If initial training for most teachers is conducted during summers, how frequently and when will follow-up coaching in classrooms occur throughout the year? What proportion of teachers are involved in collaborative problem solving, and where and when does most of their work occur?
- Be realistic about the resources you have or could likely obtain, to support estimates for time needed.
- Negotiate directly the trade-offs staff and administrators are open to—and unwilling to touch—in order to gain time for professional development.
- Involve parents and other community caregivers in discussions, particularly if your plans are likely to affect teacher contact time with children or altered school start and dismissal times. Be prepared with clear explanations of how your school's professional development goals are linked tightly to student learning priorities. Provide examples of how children are likely to benefit from teachers' increased knowledge or skills in the targeted area(s).
- Pilot any new plans for at least a year prior to committing to them. Where possible, piloting several different strategies within the same school district can produce valuable insights and comparisons of cost and benefits.

- Enlist teachers' help in communicating the value of their professional learning time to students. For example, "Today we are going to do something I learned in Study Group yesterday." Reinforcing messages like these can serve as models of lifelong learning for youth. Such messages may also make their way to families, and help build community support for the time and resources devoted to professional development.

Strategies for Making the Most of Funds

As you may recall from Chapter 4, research on what makes staff development effective points to five features: (a) focus on content knowledge, (b) collective participation, (c) use of active learning strategies, (d) coherence, and (e) duration. Collective participation and duration are the features that impact teacher time the most. And teacher time is your school's greatest cost, resource, and investment (Hornbeck, 2003; Odden, Archibald, Fermanich, & Gallagher, 2002).

Given that funding is limited in every district, this section offers five strategies for making the most out of limited professional development funds:

- Focus on fewer school improvement goals.
- Link external funds to those goals.
- Serve fewer teachers.
- Advocate assertively within your own district.
- Use existing time wisely.

Focusing on Fewer Goals

After carefully investigating the ways schools address the problem of limited teacher time, Watts and Castle (1993) conclude that "Sometimes it is better to slow down, accomplish more by attempting less, and accept the fact that you can't do it all" (p. 309). Similarly, the expert thinking synthesized in Chapters 1 and 5 underscored the importance of setting priorities, reducing fragmentation, and persistent leadership focus. For many schools, that means concentrating on fewer improvement goals, including those for teachers' professional development.

Schools stumble when their leaders cannot identify priorities, or when they seem to say "Pay attention to everything;

everything is important." . . . Six school improvement goals are not better than one. Meaningful substantive changes in schools occur through focused, concentrated efforts. (DuFour, 2002b, pp. 60–61)

It is often as difficult to trim initiatives and programs as to grow them. But trimming may be needed for a school to be able to address a few priorities deeply and well. Focusing on fewer goals can be one means of stretching scarce funds effectively.

Linking External Funds to Top-Priority Goals

Hornbeck's (2003) studies of district spending reveal that 40 to 60 percent of professional development activities are paid by external funds. The greatest sources of those funds are, typically, Title I, Eisenhower grants for math and science, and technology initiatives of various sorts. Other substantive contributors are IDEA (special education), bilingual initiatives, innovations targeted by individual states, and partnerships with universities.

The leadership challenge is to ensure that those sources' funds support and complement your school's priorities for student learning. Accomplish this by doing the following:

- Building relationships with central office or other staff responsible for applying for, dispersing, and monitoring external funds and partnerships.
- Making certain the district understands your school's improvement goals. (Again, the fewer there are, the more clearly they may be remembered.)
- Helping grant application writers identify where there is overlap between your school's priorities and the funding source's goals and restrictions.

Often, the larger the school district, the stronger the central office infrastructure for soliciting and receiving external funds. These infrastructures can become so centered on the difficult task of bringing in more dollars that they become disconnected from individual school improvement priorities. Your job as a school leader is to persuasively remind them otherwise, insisting on coherence.

Though it is easy to become seduced into thinking that "any new funding is better than none," the result may be deflection from or dilution of your school's agreed-upon targets. The desired outcome is selectively linking external funds to your school's improvement goals, so that professional development efforts do not become fragmented. As Hornbeck (2003) puts it, "Districts must move away from organizing activities around funding sources and [instead,] combine funding streams to support integrated efforts aimed at school needs" (p. 29).

Serving Fewer Teachers

When funds simply cannot support high-quality professional development for all teachers, it is better to serve fewer teachers than to sacrifice quality (Birman et al., 2000). You do not need a book to provide examples of the many unproductive staff development practices that have plagued the public schools historically. Research experts acknowledge that sustaining all quality indicators (especially duration and collective participation) is expensive (Birman et al., 2000; Odden et al., 2002). But compromising on those features in order to spread professional development across as many teachers as possible is not the answer.

The strategy of offering fewer teachers professional development opportunities can be challenging politically. Due to both tradition and collectively bargained agreements that reinforce treating all teachers the same, staff may balk at this suggestion. I would underscore two counterpoints.

First, most teachers understand that resources are limited. Accordingly, they may appreciate either of the following:

a. Your advocating directly for investing in doing professional development well for a few teachers rather than either postponing the improvement initiative or providing less effective, lower-cost forms of adult learning for all
b. The opportunity to collectively discuss and decide among the options depicted in (a) or to brainstorm additional options together

My second counterpoint is that *ineffective* staff development practices are also expensive, though the costs may be more cultural than financial. That is, low-quality professional development experiences inspire negativity among teachers who feel their time is being wasted. Negativity can be contagious, eventually affecting the overall learning climate and culture of the school.

Being Assertive Within Your Own District

In many districts, funding is not distributed equally among component schools. Each school within the district does not receive exactly the same resources for organizational improvement or staff development (Hornbeck, 2003). For example, a study of large urban districts found that professional development resources ranged from $545 to $9,000 per teacher in one district's elementary schools (Hornbeck, 2003).

Sometimes differences are due to enrollment variations, including special needs (e.g., high proportions of students from low socioeconomic levels, English language learners, or other students eligible for selected programs). Sometimes, resource differences are also related to a school's leadership history. In other words, principals' advocacy for their schools matters.

Accordingly, another strategy for optimizing resources is to be assertive within your own school district. I recommend assertiveness in the sense of self-confidence, firmness, and persistence, not pushiness or annoying aggression. How best to strike an appropriate balance?

- Be well informed and articulate about effective professional development content, processes, and contexts. (This book provides all the fundamentals.)
- Have a focused plan based on your school's agreed-upon priorities for student and adult learning. (Again, keep it short and simple.)
- Build solid relationships with your superintendent, other pertinent district-level administrators, and school board members.
- Communicate your school's resource needs clearly and regularly to those key decision makers.
- Support your requests and plans with strong rationale. (Again, this book provides all the background needed to do that well.)
- Share data and evidence of value. (This is why gap analysis and evaluation were addressed so early in this volume.)

Of course, I do not mean to promote unnecessarily competitive tactics or pitting one school against another. In fact, sharing personnel and resources with other schools within a district often makes sense. Nevertheless, uneven or inadequate resource allocations districtwide may also require strong advocacy and assertiveness by individual school leaders.

Additionally, teachers' help can be elicited to seek funds for your school's professional development from sources outside the district (Hornbeck, 2003). Where strong writing talent exists, school-based grants can be submitted to private foundations, state, or federal funding sources. You may find teachers willing to take the lead on grant writing, especially if your school supports such work as a part of Individually Guided or Collaborative Problem Solving forms of professional development. The grant writing process can be a valuable learning experience for teachers and administrators, with a happy by-product—increased funding—for the whole school.

Using Existing Time Wisely

Few schools consistently allocate *no* resources to teachers' professional development. Hence, even when no additional time or funding is available, it may still be possible to improve existing practices by applying the strategies, tools, and ideas discussed throughout this volume.

For example, there may be circumstances when just one day a year is available to your school for professional development; or when just 2 teachers out of 50 can participate in a particular training initiative; or when just a few novices are afforded mentors. It is still important to ensure that content and processes are carefully selected, that adult learning time is linked to your school's highest priority student goals, and that the everyday acts of leadership support a positive school context for teacher growth.

Doing professional development well is possible no matter how small the scale. Are individual teachers' talents being shared as broadly as possible? Is every faculty meeting used as productively as it could be? Are community services being tapped consistently? Are interns and volunteers being used as well as they could be? Are incremental improvements acknowledged and celebrated? Using existing time, personnel, and funding more effectively is another strategy for making the most of limited resources (Richardson, 2002; Watts & Castle, 1993).

An Image of Success

Admittedly, you have become a bit of a squeaky wheel at the central office when it comes to money matters. You always act professionally, of course. For example, you make sure you link

---

(Continued)

(Continued)

your requests directly to student learning data and strong instructional rationale. You are well prepared and unflappable when school board members ask tough questions about your proposals. You take no for an answer graciously, while remaining undeterred about pursuing the possible yes when additional opportunities or ideas arise. You are ever vigilant about the federal and state funds coming into the district to be sure your school is allocated its fair share.

You have two teachers dedicating their individually guided learning time to pursuing literacy grants to support the school's reading comprehension focus. They are happy to be doing so and are also earning university credit for their effort as part of a project for their advanced degrees in educational leadership. You are encouraging both to consider taking on staff developer roles in your school for their required administrative internships. They could be enormous assets in expanding the coaching help already provided to teachers.

Though it took nine months to build support for the change, the teachers' union and district have agreed to let your school pilot a restructured calendar for next year. The three professional development days already built into the annual schedule will be converted into six half-days. Your teachers felt they needed more frequent, though shorter, chunks of time interspersed throughout the year. The pilot will allow them more collective opportunities for additional training, after practicing the new reading comprehension strategies in their classrooms in five- to seven-week intervals.

Taken together, your school's modest but early success moving forward with professional development priorities is encouraging. You remain confident about the prospects for additional investments in the school's long-term improvement plans.

Summary

This chapter, together with the previous two, focused on what principals and other school leaders can do to create supportive *contexts* for teachers' professional development. Chapters 5 and 6 centered on the contextual issues of nurturing positive school climates, focusing improvement efforts, integrating innovations, facilitating change, and sustaining concentration on student learning priorities.

This chapter supplemented those broader leadership strategies with consideration of the nitty-gritty of daily schedules and funds. More specifically, this chapter suggested steps you can take to

- Find time for professional development.
- Lead processes for altering staff or student time in school.
- Make the most out of limited funds for adult learning.

Enhancing systems of support for teacher development necessarily involves attention to the technical resources of time and money, as well as the less tangible leadership skills of culture- and coherence-building. All are important elements in cultivating contexts that help, rather than hinder, your school's improvement efforts.

Next Steps

You have worked hard to lead a multiyear, collaborative effort to enhance your school's professional development practices. You have studied and applied a broad range of information derived from both research and expert consensus. Your immersion in this improvement process has kept you focused and motivated. Now you need a simple means of reinforcing what you have learned, when future derailments from best practices inevitably surface. To that end, the final chapter wraps up and reiterates several of this book's most salient themes and messages.

8

Summing Up

The previous chapters have covered considerable ground in this journey to understand and illustrate ways school leaders can support and sustain teachers' professional development. In this final chapter, I briefly do the following:

- Review the state of the art today
- Note several differences between contemporary and prior thinking
- Identify implications of those shifts for school leaders

For your future work, I encourage you to revisit this chapter whenever you have just a few moments to refresh your thoughts about the essential elements of professional development leadership.

Recap

In this section, I summarize key concepts and selected strategies that have been elaborated in previous chapters. Figure 8.1 displays many of the essential elements school leaders should understand about professional development.

Content

First and foremost, effective professional development practices are built on a foundation of solid *content*, (as represented by the shaded, three-dimensional block near the top of the oval in Figure 8.1.)

Figure 8.1 Summary of Key Concepts

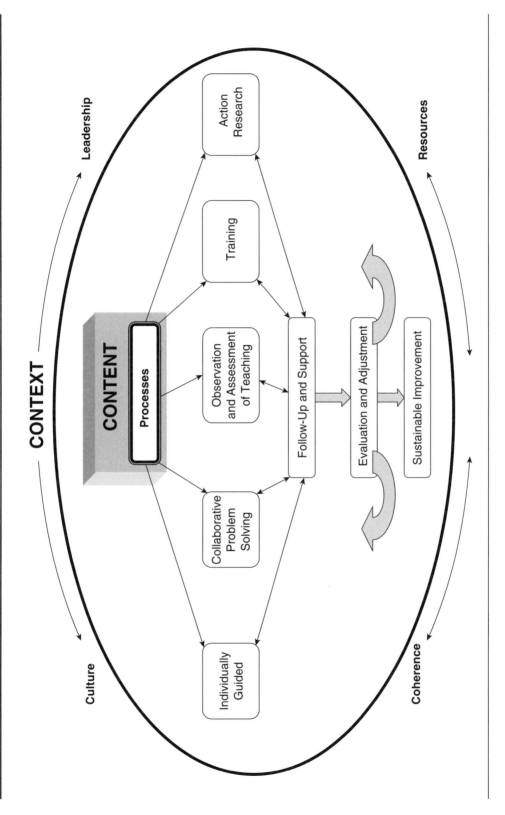

That content is grounded in the gaps in student learning you and your teachers have determined to be the highest priorities for your school to address collectively. The substance of teachers' learning is linked directly to the agreed-upon student learning priorities.

Strong school leaders reinforce the links between student and adult development every chance they get. Such reinforcement keeps improvement efforts focused and sustains momentum toward child-centered goals. Leaders also ensure that collaboratively developed evaluation questions are asked along the way. Answers to those questions are used to adjust professional development content, both in progress and for future improvement planning.

Process

How the selected content is engaged with can take many different shapes (as represented by the multiple *processes* displayed across the midsection of the oval in Figure 8.1). Volumes have been written on the myriad formats different teachers and groups have used. At their core, however, teacher learning processes can generally be classified within one of five models: Individually Guided, Collaborative Problem Solving, Observation and Assessment of Teaching, Training, and Action Research. These five conceptual handles can help you grasp the essence of particular formats popular today (e.g., lesson study, critical friends groups, cognitive coaching, teacher reflection) or that may be promoted in the future.

Strong school leaders see to it that multiple-year follow-up and support is provided, no matter what the design of the initial development effort. Through the questions they ask, the facilitators they identify, and the planning they oversee, leaders also ensure that the processes selected incorporate what is known about effective adult learning practices. Such practices typically involve active participation strategies, teacher choice, extended dialogue with peers, focus on subject matter knowledge, and relevance to current challenges. As with content, evaluation and feedback from participants should guide the redesign or modification of those processes.

Context

Both professional development content and processes are situated within a particular school *context* (as represented by the captions and arrows surrounding the oval depicted in Figure 8.1). This environment either helps or hinders collective movement toward

improvement goals. Student-centered content and exemplary professional development processes will prosper—or wither—depending
upon the overall school culture of which they are part.

Strong principals create and sustain supportive contexts for
teachers' professional development. They do so by sharing leadership
and decision making generously while maintaining focus on student-
centered goals. They make multiple development efforts cohere by
facilitating sense making of all that is going on at the school, by reinforcing connections among initiatives, and by helping map what
desired improvements look like. They foster two-way communication and respond helpfully to teacher concerns about change. They
harness the limited resources of time and funds to support a realistic
number of carefully selected improvement goals for their school.
They serve as role models of continuous learning for themselves. And
they are resiliently optimistic about what the school's students and
teachers can achieve together.

In sum, Figure 8.1 depicts the multidimensional and interdependent parts that contribute to sustainable school improvement through
professional development. This figure also provides a handy graphic
synthesis of much of the information contained in this book.

What Has Changed Over Time?

The current state of the art differs from prior thinking about professional development in several important ways (Sparks, 2002; Sparks
& Hirsch, 1997).

Accountability for Outcomes

First, greater emphasis is placed on demonstrable results today
than ever before. Moreover, the gold standard for desired results is
student learning.

In decades past, we may have been more trusting that any and all
additional teacher learning was good. After all, it seemed to make
sense that continuously learning faculty would be a greater asset than
faculty whose formal learning was static.

But today we are more concerned with *what* and *how well* teachers
are learning, and *whether* students are benefiting from teachers' professional development. Hence the current prominence of connecting
adult learning directly to students' needs and of assessing outcomes
at multiple levels. (See Chapters 1 and 2.) The emergence of national

standards for professional development is another example of today's increased emphasis on verifiable indicators of quality.

Tapping Grassroots Potential

We have also shifted from almost exclusive reliance on the Training model to valuing more diverse forms of staff development. This change has meant greater use of individualized and small-group learning formats. Sometimes these formats piggyback on initial training, and sometimes they operate as beneficial learning processes in and of themselves.

This change also reflects a shift in thinking about wherein lie the best solutions to local challenges. For example, training often involves bringing in outside consultants or noted authorities to share their knowledge. The other four models rely more heavily on independent reflection, faculty pairs, and dialogue, study, and problem solving with peers. (See Chapter 3.) In these models, teachers and teacher leaders are the experts. Adult learning initiatives are more likely to be based at the local school. And, in its ideal form, professional development is integrated within the regular workday, rather than separated as an intermittent special event.

The Power of Environment

A third difference from times past is the increased emphasis placed on the context in which professional development occurs today. On one level, this shift represents thinking more systemically about all the interrelated pieces that contribute to the whole of an individual school's trajectory.

On another, it reflects an expanded knowledge base suggesting that technical interventions alone are insufficient for achieving most schools' improvement goals. For example, even when a professional development initiative is designed and implemented technically perfectly, incorporating outstanding facilitators and the finest research on learning and follow-up, it may still fall short. The local culture, politics, human relations, resources, and leadership also impact what can be accomplished and sustained in any school.

Implications for School Leaders

What are the implications of these shifts in thinking about professional development for current and future principals?

Accountability Perspectives

On one hand, the increasing emphasis on demonstrable student outcomes puts additional pressure on all educational leaders, whether in classrooms or administrative offices. Nonetheless, the public commonly holds the building principal accountable for overall school performance. This is a weighty responsibility.

On the other hand, the press for student results also empowers principals to insist on priority setting and communal focus on goals for children's learning. Such accountability can compel greater clarity and purposefulness in short- and long-term planning and action. It can help leadership cut through the clutter of other issues that invariably appear to be urgent but—through the filter of student learning results—may actually be less central. It can clarify resource and personnel decision making and provide powerful justification for how you and your teachers choose to concentrate your collective energies.

Today's accent on tangible results also affords school leaders the opportunity to target learning goals other than students' performance on multiple-choice tests. More and more parents are voicing frustration with overly narrow assessments of their children's abilities. Data-based gap analyses can reveal all kinds of strengths and weaknesses meriting priority attention. Improvement interventions can be centered on student learning expectations that are not tested in your state (e.g., writing, applied problem solving, creative thinking, citizenship). As long as you are able to provide plausible evidence of student growth, you can both demonstrate powerful results *and* be the school you and your teachers aim to be.

Lessons From the Grassroots

What are the leadership implications of the move toward supplementing training models with more diversified adult learning processes? First is talent identification. For example, rather than looking for staff developers with the strongest presentation skills, today's principals need to be able to recognize and nurture respected collaborators. Instead of searching for those comfortable teaching large groups of professionals, we need to identify active listeners who can facilitate team problem solving. More so than exemplary communication gifts, contemporary forms of professional development require teachers with deep subject matter knowledge who are willing to share strategies with others.

Second, today's more varied processes for adult learning also suggest larger political roles for principals. That is, you must be capable of educating the community, school boards, union leadership, and (sometimes even) superintendents, about what should count as professional development. While training led by renowned experts is a familiar format, some stakeholders might not recognize or appreciate other models of adult learning. For example, though there may be a long history of compensating teachers for their completion of graduate coursework, the notion of allocating funding for action research, Saturday study groups, or individualized professional development plans will likely be questioned. Part of your job is to build political and financial support by sharing up-to-date knowledge about effective professional development practice.

Context Up Close and Personal

In large part, principals set the tone for their buildings. Additionally, they are the face of the school for key district decision makers and external publics. The values principals model, the ethics they demonstrate, the respect they earn, and the commitments that drive their workdays contribute significantly to how the school's culture is experienced and perceived. In short, principals' influence is enormous in shaping context.

This personal power means that *who you are* as a human being makes a big difference to a school. One implication of the powerful influence of this position is to be sure you *know* who you are and what you stand for. Another is to *trust* your values, ethics, and commitments. These are the intangibles that will guide you through the challenges of school improvement—and simultaneously shape the building's culture.

The Promise of Leadership for Professional Development

In this chapter, I have recapped where professional development is today, synthesized changes from earlier thinking, and identified implications of those changes for school leaders. I conclude with several final thoughts.

First, the principal's roles elaborated in this book represent key opportunities for *instructional leadership.* While much has been written about this seemingly lofty term, I think of it simply as keeping the *educational* in educational administration, the school's collective work centered on enhancing student learning, and administrative leaders' work focused on supporting children's learning through ongoing adult development and school improvement.

I challenge conventional notions about how removed educational administration is from children and classrooms. This book's many examples of how and where strong leaders intervene to impact content, processes, and context counter such misleading lore.

I remind current principals of how important their everyday acts are to both students' and teachers' school experiences. And I hope this vision of leadership inspires veteran teachers and prospective administrators to consider the principalship as a career choice for themselves.

Glossary

Action Research: A model of professional development in which individuals or groups of teachers try out (experiment with) different approaches in the classroom, collect data about the impact of their intervention, then analyze results to determine whether or how instruction might be changed for subsequent lessons. A systematic investigation and reflection process.

Alignment: A process aimed at matching or coordinating two or more elements so that they mutually support, complement, or are congruent with one another.

Assessment: A systematic process of collecting, describing, reviewing, and analyzing data from one or more sources. Results may be used to provide feedback or to make judgments about quality. See also *summative* and *formative assessment*.

Backward design or backward mapping: Planning that begins by identifying the student learning outcomes desired, then proceeds to determine the instructional, curricular, professional development, and other resources necessary to achieve those outcomes. A phrase often used synonymously is "beginning with the end in mind."

Behaviorism: A theory of learning that assumes learners are primarily motivated by rewarding desired behaviors and sanctioning incorrect or undesirable performances. Often contrasted with *constructivism*.

Cognitive coaching: A structured process in which an observer asks probing, open-ended questions to elicit a teacher's sense making and self-analysis of observed lesson(s). The goal is to foster teachers' abilities to clarify or make changes in their own thinking, decision making, and teaching. In contrast to most peer coaching, the observer's role is

---

NOTE: Terms are defined as they apply to teachers' professional development.

to facilitate the teacher's analyses, rather than to provide feedback or interpretation of what occurred in the classroom. A form of the Observation and Assessment model of professional development.

Collaborative Problem Solving: A model of professional development in which two or more teachers work together to address issues of common concern and, in the process, learn from and with each other. Takes many different forms, including, for example, curriculum development, school improvement planning, critical friends, study groups, mentoring, and lesson study.

Concept map: See *graphic organizer*.

Concerns-Based Adoption Model (CBAM): A system for supporting the implementation of an educational change by recognizing, monitoring, and responding to teachers' reactions and challenges related to the change.

Constructivism: A theory of teaching and learning that views students as active creators of their own learning with others, rather than passive recipients of knowledge transmitted by others. Typically centers on building upon the learner's prior knowledge, experience, and interests. Often contrasted with *behaviorism*.

Content: The knowledge, skills, and attitudes that are the substance or subject matter of teachers' learning. *What* is to be learned. One of three critical components of national standards for staff development aimed at improving student learning.

Context: The organizational, systemic environment of which professional development is a part. One of three critical components of national standards for staff development aimed at improving student learning.

Critical friends: A structured group process for providing support, feedback, and opportunities for reflection and challenge among colleagues. Its purpose is to improve instruction and student learning. A form of the Collaborative Problem Solving model of professional development.

Curriculum: What is taught to students: both intended and unintended information, skills, and attitudes.

Curriculum mapping: A collaborative process of describing the substance, sequence, and/or amount of time spent teaching a subject, skill, objective, or behavior. May be used for diagnosing, coordinating, or planning improvements needed.

Data: Systematically gathered facts, figures, records, reports, observations, or other information from which conclusions may be drawn.

Differentiated instruction: Teachers' adaptations (modifications) of curricula, instruction, assessment, or expected student products aimed at addressing children's diverse learning styles, readiness, abilities, or interests.

Disaggregated data: Data sorted, categorized, and analyzed by demographic or other subgroups. Examples of subgroupings include sex, socioeconomic status, race, ethnicity, grade level, and special needs.

Evaluation: A systematic process of gathering, reviewing, and analyzing data from multiple sources in order to make a judgment about value, worth, or quality in relation to established criteria. Often used synonymously with *summative assessment*. Contrast with *formative assessment*.

Evidence: Data that serve to answer an evaluation question and support findings about the quality of professional development.

Formative assessment: A process of gathering data and providing feedback on teaching or learning in relation to established criteria or standards. Used to help students or teachers grow, to guide instruction, or to improve future performance, rather than to rate or judge quality, worth, value, or potential at a particular moment in time. Contrast with *summative assessment*.

Graphic organizer: A visual aid designed to display and clarify information in simple, summary terms. Common examples include diagrams, flow charts, concept maps, tables, and figures of various sorts.

Individually Guided: A model of professional development in which teachers determine the goals, content, and processes for their own learning. Examples of Individually Guided activities include reading, journaling, writing for publication, creating a teaching portfolio, or attending a professional conference.

Individual professional development plan: A document teachers write to delineate their learning and growth goals, as well as the action steps to be taken to attain those goals. A form of the Individually Guided model of professional development.

Innovation Configurations Map: A continuum that (a) identifies the critical components of a particular educational innovation, and (b) describes them in their ideal state as well as in their varied forms (configurations) of implementation apart from the ideal. A means of sharing what a planned change "looks like," and a tool for diagnosing and monitoring progress toward enacting the change in practice.

Learning communities: Reflective, collaborative environments where teachers and administrators work together to increase student learning, enhance teachers' practices, and improve schools. Also refers to collegial groups in which members commit to ongoing learning and mutual assistance.

Mentoring: A paired process in which a more experienced teacher assists and guides a less experienced one. A form of the Collaborative Problem Solving model of professional development.

Model: A pattern or plan that guides the design of a professional development program.

Observation: A data collection technique in which the collector is in a position to witness the actions, hear the words, and experience the classroom atmosphere of a particular teacher during instruction.

Observation and Assessment of Teaching: A model of professional development in which teachers visit each other's classrooms, make notes of what occurs, and analyze the observed instruction through reflective discussion afterwards. The goal is for both to learn from the process of holding up a mirror to teachers' and students' classroom behaviors.

One-legged interview: A data collection technique in which a change facilitator conducts an informal, brief discussion with a teacher concerning the implementation of a planned change. One of several tools part of the Concerns-Based Adoption Model (CBAM) for improving schools.

Peer coaching: A structured process in which pairs of teachers observe each other in the classroom and provide feedback to one another in order to improve or refine instruction and student learning. A form of the Observation and Assessment model of professional development.

Portfolio: A collection of artifacts and written reflections that demonstrate evidence of a teacher's knowledge, skills, and growth over time. The process of selecting sample work and constructing the collection is often considered as important as the product itself. A form of the Individually Guided model of professional development.

Process: The ways that teachers engage with professional development content. *How* opportunities for learning are designed. *Process* is often used interchangeably with terms such as format, program, models, approach, delivery, or activities. One of three critical components of national standards for staff development aimed at improving student learning.

Protocols: Discussion guides. Outlines that define, sequence, and time procedures designed to inspire dialogue and reflection among small groups of teachers. A protocol's purpose is to organize and structure discussions often when examining lessons or samples of student work together. Sometimes referred to as *tuning protocols*.

Qualitative data: Information that is expressed in words (rather than numbers). Qualitative research often relies on interviews, observations, and documents as its primary sources of data.

Quantitative data: Information that is expressed in numbers (rather than words) and can be analyzed statistically.

Root cause analysis: Intense probing to uncover the source(s) of a problem or undesirable result. As potential sources are identified, additional *why* questions are raised, to determine if anything lies even deeper beneath initial conjectures about what is primarily responsible for the problem.

Rubric: An assessment tool. A continuum that describes a range of performance levels for each of several specific elements of the performance. Sometimes used to distinguish levels of progress toward desired outcomes (i.e., for formative assessment). Frequently used to rate performance from the unacceptable to the outstanding (i.e., for summative assessment).

Stages of Concern: A diagnostic tool used in the Concerns-Based Adoption Model (CBAM) that identifies varied levels of feelings that teachers often experience when an educational change is expected.

Standards: Statements that identify the essential knowledge, skills, behaviors, or other attributes desired. Verbs often begin these statements (e.g., knows, uses, applies, provides, demonstrates, is able to). Standards typically identify what good teachers (or students) should know and be able to do. Professional development standards identify the attributes of high-quality content, processes, and context.

Study groups: A small-group or whole-school process wherein teachers meet regularly over an extended period of time to learn together about a topic of mutual interest. Topics and degree of structure for the process vary widely. Collegial reflection and discussion are always expected. A form of the Collaborative Problem Solving model of professional development.

Summative assessment: A judgment about the quality, value, or worth of teaching performance or potential (e.g., unsatisfactory, satisfactory, exemplary) in relation to established criteria or standards and at a particular moment in time. Typically used for high-stakes decision making about hiring, tenure, merit raises, dismissal, annual reviews, and the like. Contrast with *formative assessment*.

TESA: Acronym for Teacher Expectations and Student Achievement. A particular training program aimed at increasing teachers' awareness of the ways they interact with students. Program's goal is to enhance equitable interactions by sex, race, ability, and other differences so as to improve student learning.

Title I: A common, shorthand reference to a particular part of the federal law initiated as the Elementary and Secondary Education Act of 1964 (and reauthorized in 2001 as No Child Left Behind). Although specific requirements have varied since its inception, the act typically funds and monitors educational programs aimed at improving the achievement of poor, minority, and other disadvantaged children.

Training: A model of professional development in which experts help teachers acquire new skills by: (a) presenting the skill's rationale, (b) demonstrating the skill, (c) creating opportunities for teachers to practice the new skill and receive feedback on their practice, and (d) providing follow-up guidance and assistance to teachers using the new skill in the classroom over an extended period of time.

References

Bambino, D. (2002). Critical friends. *Educational Leadership, 59*(6), 25–27.

Beane, J. (2002). A democratic core curriculum. *Educational Leadership, 59*(7), 25–28.

Birman, B., Desimone, L., Porter, A., & Garet, M. (2000). Designing professional development that works. *Educational Leadership, 57*(8), 28–33.

Briggs, K., & Myers, I. (1987). *Myers-Briggs Type Indicator–Form G.* Palo Alto, CA: Consulting Psychologists.

Brooks, J., & Brooks, M. (1999). *In search of understanding: The case for constructivist classrooms.* Alexandria, VA: Association for Supervision and Curriculum Development.

Burnette, B. (2002). How we formed our community. *Journal of Staff Development, 23*(1), 51–54.

Conners, G. (2000). *Good news: How to get the best possible media coverage for your school.* Thousand Oaks, CA: Corwin.

Costa, A., & Garmston, R. (1994). *Cognitive coaching.* Norwood, MA: Christopher Gordon.

Covey, S. (1989). *The seven habits of highly effective people.* New York: Simon & Schuster.

Dana, N., & Yendol-Silva, D. (2003). *The reflective educator's guide to classroom research.* Thousand Oaks, CA: Corwin.

Deal, T., & Peterson, K. (1999). *Shaping school culture: The heart of leadership.* San Francisco: Jossey-Bass.

DuFour, R. (2001). In the right context. *Journal of Staff Development, 22*(1), 14–17.

DuFour, R. (2002a). How to get the best return on the minute. *Journal of Staff Development, 23*(1), 60–61.

DuFour, R. (2002b). One clear voice is needed in the din. *Journal of Staff Development, 23*(2), 60–61.

English, F. (2000). *Deciding what to teach and test: Developing, aligning, and auditing the curriculum.* Thousand Oaks, CA: Corwin.

Fullan, M. (1991). *The new meaning of educational change.* New York: Teachers College Press.

Fullan, M. (2000). The three stories of education reform. *Phi Delta Kappan, 81*(8), 581–584.

Fullan, M. (2001). *The new meaning of educational change* (3rd ed.). New York: Teachers College Press.

Garet, M., Birman, B., Porter, A., Desimone, L., & Herman, B. (with Suk Yoon, K.). (1999). *Designing effective professional development: Lessons from the Eisenhower Program.* Washington, DC: U.S. Department of Education.

Glatthorn, A. (1997). *Differentiated supervision* (2nd ed.). Alexandria, VA: Association for Supervision and Curriculum Development.

Glickman, C. (2002). *Leadership for learning: How to help teachers succeed.* Alexandria, VA: Association for Supervision and Curriculum Development.

Glickman, C., Gordon, S., & Ross-Gordon, J. (2001). *Supervision and instructional leadership: A developmental approach.* Needham Heights, MA: Allyn & Bacon.

Gordon, S. (2004). *Professional development for school improvement: Empowering learning communities.* Boston: Pearson Education–Allyn & Bacon.

Gregorc, A. (1982). *Gregorc style delineator.* Columbia, CT: Gregorc Associates.

Guskey, T. (1997). Putting it all together: Integrating educational innovations. In S. Caldwell (Ed.), *Professional development in learning-centered schools* (pp. 130–161). Oxford, OH: National Staff Development Council.

Guskey, T. (2000). *Evaluating professional development.* Thousand Oaks, CA: Corwin.

Guskey, T. (2002). Does it make a difference? Evaluating professional development. *Educational Leadership, 59*(6), 45–51.

Guskey, T. (2003a). Analyzing lists of the characteristics of effective professional development to promote visionary leadership. *NASSP Bulletin, 87*(637), 4–20.

Guskey, T. (2003b). Scooping up meaningful evidence. *Journal of Staff Development, 24*(4), 27–30.

Guskey, T. (2003c). What makes professional development effective? *Phi Delta Kappan, 84*(10), 748–750.

Hall, G., & Hord, S. (1987). *Change in schools: Facilitating the process.* Albany, NY: State University of New York Press.

Hall, G., & Hord, S. (2001). *Implementing change: Patterns, principles, and potholes.* Boston: Allyn & Bacon.

Holloway, J. (2003). Linking professional development to student learning. *Educational Leadership, 61*(3), 85–87.

Holloway, K. (2003, February/March). A measure of concern. *Tools for Schools,* 1–6.

Hord, S., Rutherford, W., Huling-Austin, L., & Hall, G. (1987). *Taking charge of change.* Alexandria, VA: Association for Supervision and Curriculum Development.

Hornbeck, M. (2003). What your district's budget is telling you. *Journal of Staff Development, 24*(3), 28–32.

Janas, M. (1998). Shhh, the dragon is asleep and its name is resistance. *Journal of Staff Development, 19*(3), 10–12.

Joyce, B., & Showers, B. (1995). *Student achievement through staff development* (2nd ed.). White Plains, NY: Longman.

Joyce, B., & Showers, B. (2002). *Student achievement through staff development* (3rd ed.). Alexandria, VA: Association for Supervision and Curriculum Development.

Killion, J. (2002). *Assessing impact: Evaluating staff development.* Oxford, OH: National Staff Development Council.

Kinder, J. (2000). *A short guide to school public relations.* Bloomington, IN: Phi Delta Kappa Educational Foundation.

Kirkpatrick, D. L. (1959). Techniques for evaluating training programs. *Training and Development Journal, 13*(11), 11–16.

Kirkpatrick, D. L. (1977). Evaluating training programs: Evidence versus proof. *Training and Development Journal, 31*(11), 9–12.

Kirkpatrick, D. L. (1998). *Evaluating training programs: The four levels* (2nd ed.). San Francisco: Berrett-Kohler.

Knowles, M., Holton, E., & Swanson, R. (1998). *The adult learner.* Newton, MA: Butterworth-Heinemann.

Lambert, L. (1998). *Building leadership capacity in schools.* Alexandria, VA: Association for Supervision and Curriculum Development.

Langer, G., Colter, A., & Goff, L. (2003). *Collaborative analysis of student work: Improving teaching and learning.* Alexandria, VA: Association for Supervision and Curriculum Development.

Lindstrom, P., & Speck, M. (2004). *The principal as professional development leader.* Thousand Oaks, CA: Corwin.

Marzano, R., Pickering, D., & Brandt, R. (1990). Integrating instructional programs through dimensions of learning. *Educational Leadership, 47*(5), 17–24.

McTighe, J., & Thomas, R. (2003). Backward design for forward action. *Educational Leadership, 60*(5), 52–55.

Murphy, C., & Lick, D. (2001). *Whole faculty study groups: Creating student based staff development* (2nd ed.). Thousand Oaks, CA: Corwin.

National Staff Development Council (NSDC). (2001). *NSDC Standards for staff development.* Retrieved January 12, 2004, from www.nsdc.org/standards/about

National Staff Development Council (NSDC). (2004). *About NSDC.* Retrieved February 19, 2004, from www.nsdc.org/connect/about/faqs

Nevills, P. (2003). Cruising the cerebral superhighway. *Journal of Staff Development, 24*(1), 20–23.

Newmann, F., Smith, B., Allensworth, E., & Bryk, A. (2001). Instructional program coherence: What it is and why it should guide school improvement policy. *Educational Evaluation and Policy Analysis, 23*(4), 297–321.

No Child Left Behind Act (NCLB). (2001). Public law #107–110. Retrieved February 3, 2004, from www.ed.gov/legislation/ESEA02

Odden, A., Archibald, S., Fermanich, M., & Gallagher, A. (2002). How to figure the cost of professional development. *Journal of Staff Development, 23*(2), 53–58.

Peterson, K. (2002). Positive or negative. *Journal of Staff Development, 23*(3), 10–15.

Portner, H. (2003). *Mentoring new teachers* (updated ed.). Thousand Oaks, CA: Corwin.

Richardson, J. (2001a, February/March). Group wise: Strategies for examining student work together. *Tools for Schools Newsletter,* 1–6.

Richardson, J. (2001b, October/November). Seeing through new eyes: Walk throughs offer new way to view schools. *Tools for Schools Newsletter,* 1–4.

Richardson, J. (2002, August/September). Think outside the clock: Create time for professional learning. *Tools for Schools Newsletter,* 1–7.

Richardson, J. (2004, February/March). Lesson study: Teachers learn how to improve instruction. *Tools for Schools Newsletter,* 1–8.

Roberts, S., & Pruitt, E. (2003). *Schools as professional learning communities: Collaborative activities and strategies for professional development.* Thousand Oaks, CA: Corwin.

Roy, P., & Hord, S. (2003). *Moving NSDC's staff development standards into practice: Innovation configurations.* Oxford, OH: National Staff Development Council and Southwest Educational Development Laboratory.

Schmoker, M. (2002). Up and away. *Journal of Staff Development, 23*(2), 10–13.

Schmoker, M. (2003). First things first: Demystifying data analysis. *Educational Leadership, 60*(5), 22–24.

Schmoker, M. (2004). Tipping point: From feckless reform to substantive instructional improvement. *Phi Delta Kappan, 85*(6), 424–432.

Silver, H., Strong, R., & Perini, M. (2000). *So each may learn: Integrating learning styles and multiple intelligences.* Alexandria, VA: Association for Supervision and Curriculum Development.

Sparks, D. (2002). *Designing powerful professional development for teachers and principals.* Oxford, OH: National Staff Development Council.

Sparks, D., & Hirsch, S. (1997). *A new vision for staff development.* Oxford, OH: National Staff Development Council.

Sparks, D., & Loucks-Horsley, S. (1990). Models of staff development. In R. Houston (Ed.), *Handbook of research on teacher education* (pp. 234–250). New York: Macmillan.

Sprenger, M. (2003). *Differentiation through learning styles and memory.* Thousand Oaks, CA: Corwin.

Strong, R., Silver, H., & Perini, M. (2001). Making students as important as standards. *Educational Leadership, 59*(3), 56–61.

Sullivan, S., & Glanz, J. (2000). *Supervision that improves teaching: Strategies and techniques.* Thousand Oaks, CA: Corwin.

Walsh, J., Sattes, B., & Wiman, E. (2001). A quickie checkup: Gauging continuous school improvement. *Phi Delta Kappan, 82*(7), 547–549.

Watts, G., & Castle, S. (1993). The time dilemma in school restructuring. *Phi Delta Kappan, 75*(4), 306–311.

Wiggins, G., & McTighe, J. (1998). *Understanding by design.* Alexandria, VA: Association for Supervision and Curriculum Development.

York-Barr, J., Sommers, W., Ghere, G., & Montie, J. (2001). *Reflective practice to improve schools.* Thousand Oaks, CA: Corwin.

Zeichner, K. (1999). *Teacher research as a professional development activity for P-12 educators.* Washington, DC: U.S. Department of Education.

Zmuda, A., Kuklis, R., & Kline, E. (2004). *Transforming schools: Creating a culture of continuous improvement.* Alexandria, VA: Association for Supervision and Curriculum Development.

Index

**CORWIN
PRESS**

The Corwin Press logo—a raven striding across an open book—represents the union of courage and learning. Corwin Press is committed to improving education for all learners by publishing books and other professional development resources for those serving the field of K–12 education. By providing practical, hands-on materials, Corwin Press continues to carry out the promise of its motto: **"Helping Educators Do Their Work Better."**